Nicole Johnson's

Diabetes

recipe makeovers

Publications International, Ltd.

Louis Weber, CEO
Publications International, Ltd.
7373 North Cicero Avenue
Lincolnwood, IL 60712

Photography on the cover and pages 4 and 5 by Kristi Stiff, www.kristiinc.com.

Photography on pages 9, 23, 25, 31, 33, 43, 51, 56, 73, 83, 85, 102, 103, 111, 114, 115, 117, 155, 157, and 185 by PIL Photo Studio.

Photographer: Tate Hunt
Photographer's Assistant: Justin Paris
Prop Stylist: Paula Walters
Food Stylists: Kim Loughlin, Josephine Orba
Assistant Food Stylists: Sheila Grannen, Breana Moeller

Pictured on the front cover: Café Mocha Cupcakes (*page 152*).

Pictured on the back cover (clockwise from top): Flourless Chocolate Cake (*page 166*), Prosciutto- Wrapped Chicken with Goat Cheese (*page 51*), and Cool Gelatin Dessert (*page 155*).

ISBN-13: 978-1-4508-0901-6
ISBN-10: 1-4508-0901-4

Library of Congress Control Number: 2010931042

Manufactured in China.

Nutritional Analysis: Every effort has been made to check the accuracy of the nutritional information that appears with each recipe. However, because numerous variables account for a wide range of values for certain foods, nutritive analyses in this book should be considered approximate. Different results may be obtained by using different nutrient databases and different brand-name products.

Microwave Cooking: Microwave ovens vary in wattage. Use the cooking times as guidelines and check for doneness before adding more time.

8 7 6 5 4 3 2 1

Contents

In 1993, when I was diagnosed with diabetes, I was told everything I couldn't do and everything I couldn't eat. I didn't hear much about possibility. This book is put together to show you the possibilities that exist in life with diabetes. We can enjoy great food! We can enjoy wonderful family dinners! We don't have to live a life of restrictions and negative limits! We can eat more than chicken and broccoli!

Diabetes is a challenge, no doubt. It is difficult. It can be wearisome. It can be depressing. However, our reality has a lot to do with our mindset. As you read and enjoy the things presented in this book, I urge you to consider ways to impact your own reality for the better. What can you try that might enhance your health more today than yesterday? What might you change in your routine that could improve your family's health? What could you shift in your perceptions about living with diabetes to empower you and your family to cope more fully?

Diabetes is a family condition. It impacts everyone in the family unit—both physically and mentally. I like to call the family members "Type 3s" because I believe they too live with diabetes and have their own challenges related to the condition. Often, it is the connection with loved ones in the face of challenge that makes us stronger and empowers us so we can achieve.

I try to constantly reinforce in my home that living healthy is fun. My daughter and I talk openly about my diabetes, her concerns, my concerns, and why we choose to live in certain ways. We cook together, walk together, and play together. It is a habit. (She has been known to even pretend to have diabetes!)

The best part is that she knows her mom is not defeated by disease. We fight

my diabetes together, and that togetherness is a beautiful ointment and a special treasure.

I made a promise as Miss America 1999 to fight for people with diabetes. Today, I continue to do that by finding creative ways to encourage people to see that diabetes doesn't have to stop dreams. When I was diagnosed, I was told that diabetes would keep me from an education, an aggressive career, Miss America, and certainly motherhood, but my life has proven that advice wrong. Diabetes has not been strong enough to hold me back, and I hope that you will find the strength and empowerment to beat it too!

Warmly,

Nicole Johnson

Nicole Johnson holds an MA in Journalism and an MPH with a concentration in Behavioral Science. She is pursuing a doctorate in Public Health. Nicole works at the University of South Florida as the Executive Director of Bringing Science Home and is a well-known public speaker. To learn more, visit www.NicoleJohnson.com.

Begin with Breakfast

French Toast Sticks

Using egg substitute instead of regular eggs makes this a virtually cholesterol-free recipe.

1 cup cholesterol free egg substitute

⅓ cup fat-free (skim) milk or soymilk

1 teaspoon ground cinnamon

1 teaspoon vanilla

1 round loaf unsliced peasant-style whole-grain bread

1 tablespoon reduced-fat margarine, divided

1 teaspoon powdered sugar

¼ cup sugar-free maple syrup

1. Combine egg substitute, milk, cinnamon and vanilla in large bowl.

2. Cut bread into 12 (4×1×1-inch) pieces.

3. Melt margarine in large nonstick griddle or in nonstick skillet over medium-high heat. Dip bread sticks in egg mixture to coat. Transfer to griddle. Cook sticks until golden brown on both sides. Dust lightly with powdered sugar and serve with syrup.

MAKES 4 SERVINGS
(3 TOAST STICKS WITH 1 TABLESPOON SYRUP PER SERVING)

Calories: 326, Total Fat: 8 g, Saturated Fat: <1 g, Protein: 19 g, Carbohydrate: 52 g, Cholesterol: <1 mg, Fiber: 13 g, Sodium: 457 mg

Dietary Exchanges: ½ Fat, 1 Meat, 3½ Starch

Crustless Salmon & Broccoli Quiche

Eliminating a crust on this quiche reduces fat, carbohydrates, and calories.

¾ cup cholesterol-free egg substitute

¼ cup chopped green onions

¼ cup plain fat-free yogurt

2 teaspoons all-purpose flour

1 teaspoon dried basil

⅛ teaspoon salt

⅛ teaspoon black pepper

¾ cup frozen broccoli florets, thawed and drained

⅓ cup (3 ounces) canned salmon packed in water, drained and flaked

2 tablespoons grated Parmesan cheese

1 plum tomato, thinly sliced

¼ cup fresh bread crumbs

1. Preheat oven to 375°F. Spray 1½-quart casserole or 9-inch deep-dish pie plate with nonstick cooking spray.

2. Combine egg substitute, green onions, yogurt, flour, basil, salt and pepper in medium bowl until well blended. Stir in broccoli, salmon and cheese. Spread evenly in prepared casserole. Top with tomato slices and sprinkle with bread crumbs.

3. Bake, uncovered, 20 to 25 minutes or until knife inserted into center comes out clean. Let stand 5 minutes. Cut in half before serving.

MAKES 4 SERVINGS

Calories: 227
Total Fat: 6 g
Saturated Fat: 2 g
Protein: 25 g
Carbohydrate: 20 g
Cholesterol: 25 mg
Fiber: 5 g
Sodium: 717 mg

Dietary Exchanges:
½ Fat, 2 Meat,
1 Vegetable, 1 Starch

Oatmeal with Apples and Cottage Cheese

Instead of sugary toppings, this traditional oatmeal is flavored with apples and topped with chopped pecans or almonds.

½ cup uncooked oats

½ cup diced apple

⅔ cup water

½ cup low-fat (1%) cottage cheese

¾ teaspoon ground cinnamon

1 teaspoon vanilla

Dash salt (optional)

¼ cup fat-free half-and-half

2 tablespoons chopped pecans or almonds

1½ tablespoons sugar substitute*

*This recipe was tested using sucralose-based sugar substitute.

Combine first 7 ingredients in large microwave-safe bowl and stir. Cover with wet towel and microwave on HIGH 2 minutes and then let stand 2 minutes. Add remaining ingredients, stir to combine and serve.

MAKES 2 SERVINGS

Calories: 205, Total Fat: 7 g, Saturated Fat: 1 g, Protein: 11 g, Carbohydrate: 25 g, Cholesterol: 4 mg, Dietary Fiber: 4 g, Sodium: 275 mg

Dietary Exchanges: 1 Fat, 1½ Starch

Iced Cappuccino

Substituting chocolate syrup with unsweetened cocoa powder reduces calories and carbohydrates.

1 cup vanilla fat-free frozen yogurt or vanilla fat-free ice cream

1 cup cold strong brewed coffee

1 packet sugar substitute*

1 teaspoon unsweetened cocoa powder

1 teaspoon vanilla

*This recipe was tested using sucralose-based sugar substitute.

1. Place all ingredients in food processor or blender; process until smooth. Place container in freezer; freeze 1½ to 2 hours or until top and sides of mixture are partially frozen.

2. Scrape sides of container; process until smooth and frothy. Garnish as desired. Serve immediately.

Tip: To add an extra flavor boost to this refreshing drink, add orange peel, lemon peel, or a dash of ground cinnamon to your coffee grounds before brewing.

MAKES 2 SERVINGS

Calories: 105
Total Fat: <1 g
Saturated Fat: <1 g
Protein: 5 g
Carbohydrate: 21 g
Cholesterol: <1 mg
Fiber: 0 g
Sodium: 72 mg

Dietary Exchanges:
1½ Starch

Egg and Green Chile Rice Casserole

Low-fat cheese makes this dish nearly saturated fat-free.

¾ **cup uncooked instant brown rice**

½ **cup chopped green onions**

½ **teaspoon ground cumin**

1 **can (4 ounces) chopped mild green chiles, drained**

⅛ **teaspoon salt**

1 **cup cholesterol-free egg substitute**

½ **cup (2 ounces) shredded reduced-fat sharp Cheddar cheese or Mexican cheese blend**

¼ **cup pico de gallo**

1 **medium lime, quartered**

1. Preheat oven to 350°F. Lightly coat 8-inch square baking dish with nonstick cooking spray.

2. Cook rice according to package directions. Remove from heat; stir in green onions and cumin. Transfer to prepared baking dish.

3. Sprinkle chiles and salt evenly over rice mixture. Pour egg substitute evenly over top. Bake 30 to 35 minutes or until center is set.

4. Sprinkle with cheese. Bake 3 minutes or until cheese is melted. Let stand 5 minutes before cutting into 4 squares. Serve with 1 tablespoon pico de gallo and lime wedges.

Tip: If you wish, you can further reduce the amount of sodium in this recipe by rinsing the chiles in a fine-meshed strainer before topping them onto the rice mixture.

MAKES
4 SERVINGS

Calories: 218
Total Fat: 4 g
Saturated Fat: 2 g
Protein: 14 g
Carbohydrate: 33 g
Cholesterol: 10 mg
Fiber: 2 g
Sodium: 491 mg

Dietary Exchanges:
1 Meat, 2 Starch

Nutmeg Pancakes with Lemon-Spiked Berries

Nonfat buttermilk makes this a lower-fat version of a traditional pancake recipe.

1 cup all-purpose flour

2 tablespoons sugar substitute,* divided

1 teaspoon baking powder

¾ teaspoon ground nutmeg

½ teaspoon baking soda

¼ teaspoon salt

1⅓ cups nonfat buttermilk

¼ cup cholesterol-free egg substitute

2 tablespoons canola oil

2 cups sliced strawberries

2 teaspoons grated lemon peel

This recipe was tested using sucralose-based sugar substitute.

1. Combine flour, 1 tablespoon sugar substitute, baking powder, nutmeg, baking soda and salt in medium bowl. Combine buttermilk, egg substitute and oil in small bowl. Add to flour mixture; stir just until moistened.

2. Lightly spray nonstick griddle with nonstick cooking spray; heat over medium-high heat. For each pancake, pour about ¼ cup batter onto hot griddle. Cook until top is covered with bubbles and edge is slightly dry. Turn pancake; cook until done.

3. Meanwhile, combine strawberries, remaining 1 tablespoon sugar substitute and lemon peel in medium bowl. Serve strawberry mixture over warm pancakes.

MAKES 6 SERVINGS
(1 PANCAKE WITH ⅓ CUP STRAWBERRY MIXTURE PER SERVING)

Calories: 162, Total Fat: 5 g, Saturated Fat: 1 g, Protein: 5 g, Carbohydrate: 23 g, Cholesterol: 2 mg, Fiber: 2 g, Sodium: 361 mg

Dietary Exchanges: 1 Fat, 1 Fruit, 1 Starch

Banana-Pineapple Breakfast Shake

Fat-free yogurt cuts back on the fat and calories while still adding plenty of protein.

- 2 cups plain fat-free yogurt
- 1 can (8 ounces) crushed pineapple in juice, undrained
- 1 medium ripe banana
- 8 packets sugar substitute*
- 1 teaspoon vanilla
- ⅛ teaspoon ground nutmeg
- 1 cup ice cubes

*This recipe was tested using sucralose-based sugar substitute.

1. Place all ingredients in food processor or blender; process until smooth.

2. Pour into 4 glasses. Serve immediately.

Tip: *This recipe is perfect for a brunch, a party, or another special occasion. Make as many batches as you need to serve everyone.*

MAKES 4 SERVINGS
(1 CUP PER SERVING)

Calories: 140, Total Fat: <1 g, Saturated Fat: <1 g, Protein: 8 g, Carbohydrate: 27 g, Cholesterol: 2 mg, Fiber: 1 g, Sodium: 95 mg

Dietary Exchanges: 1½ Fruit, ½ Milk

Lemon Blueberry Loaf Cake

Sugar substitute lessens the carbohydrates but keeps the same great taste.

2 cups all-purpose flour

⅓ cup granulated sugar

¼ cup instant dry milk powder

3 tablespoons sugar substitute,* divided

1 teaspoon baking powder

1 teaspoon baking soda

¼ teaspoon ground nutmeg

¼ teaspoon salt

¾ cup buttermilk or plain low-fat yogurt

2 eggs, lightly beaten

⅓ cup canola oil

3 tablespoons lemon juice

2 teaspoons grated lemon peel

1 cup fresh or frozen blueberries (do not thaw if frozen)

This recipe was tested using sucralose-based sugar substitute.

1. Preheat oven to 350°F. Grease 8×4-inch loaf pan.

2. Combine flour, granulated sugar, milk powder, 2 tablespoons sugar substitute, baking powder, baking soda, nutmeg and salt in large bowl. Combine buttermilk, eggs, oil, lemon juice and lemon peel in medium bowl until well blended. Add buttermilk mixture to flour mixture; stir just until blended.

3. Toss blueberries with remaining sugar substitute; gently fold into batter. Pour batter into prepared pan.

4. Bake 45 to 48 minutes or until toothpick inserted into center comes out clean. Cool 20 minutes in pan on wire rack. Remove cake from pan; cool completely on wire rack.

MAKES 12 SERVINGS

Calories: 180, Total Fat: 7 g, Saturated Fat: 1 g, Protein: 4 g, Carbohydrate: 25 g, Cholesterol: 35 mg, Fiber: 1 g, Sodium: 220 mg

Dietary Exchanges: 1 Fat, 1½ Starch

Brown Sugar-Cinnamon English Muffin French Toast

Using English muffins cuts calories and adds fiber to this lighter French toast recipe.

1 egg

2 egg whites

¼ cup low-fat (1%) milk

2 tablespoons light brown sugar

1 teaspoon ground cinnamon

⅛ teaspoon salt

4 whole wheat English muffins, split

8 tablespoons sugar-free pancake syrup

1 cup sliced strawberries (optional)

1. Combine egg, egg whites, milk, brown sugar, cinnamon and salt in large shallow dish; whisk until sugar dissolves. Place muffin halves in egg mixture and turn to coat; let stand about 5 minutes or until most of egg mixture is absorbed.

2. Coat large skillet with nonstick cooking spray; heat over medium heat. Add 4 muffin halves and cook, turning once, 2 to 3 minutes on each side or until lightly browned. Repeat with remaining 4 muffin halves. Serve toast topped with syrup and strawberries, if desired.

MAKES 4 SERVINGS

(1 MUFFIN WITH 2 TABLESPOONS SYRUP PER SERVING)

Calories: 203
Total Fat: 3 g
Saturated Fat: 1 g
Protein: 10 g
Carbohydrate: 38 g
Cholesterol: 54 mg
Fiber: 5 g
Sodium: 517 mg

Dietary Exchanges:
1 Meat, 2 Starch

Ham & Egg Breakfast Panini 🌾

Lean ham helps to keep fat and calories low.

¼ cup chopped green or red bell pepper

2 tablespoons sliced green onions

1 slice (1 ounce) reduced-fat smoked deli ham, chopped (¼ cup)

½ cup cholesterol-free egg substitute

Black pepper

4 slices multigrain or whole-grain bread

Nonstick cooking spray

2 (¾-ounce) slices reduced-fat Cheddar cheese or Swiss cheese

1. Coat small skillet with nonstick cooking spray; heat over medium heat. Add bell pepper and green onions; cook and stir 4 minutes or until vegetables begin to soften. Stir in ham.

2. Combine egg substitute and black pepper in small bowl; pour into skillet. Cook about 2 minutes, stirring occasionally, until egg mixture is almost set.

3. Heat grill pan or medium skillet over medium heat. Spray one side of each bread slice with cooking spray; turn bread over. Top each of 2 bread slices with 1 slice cheese and half of egg mixture. Top with remaining bread slices.

4. Grill sandwiches about 2 minutes per side, pressing sandwiches lightly with spatula, until toasted. (If desired, cover pan with lid during last 2 minutes of cooking to melt cheese.) Cut sandwiches in half; serve immediately.

MAKES 2 SERVINGS

(1 SANDWICH PER SERVING)

Calories: 271
Total Fat: 5 g
Saturated Fat: 1 g
Protein: 24 g
Carbohydrate: 30 g
Cholesterol: 9 mg
Fiber: 6 g
Sodium: 577 mg

Dietary Exchanges:
2 Meat, 2 Starch

French Toast with Sweet Butter and Orange-Spiked Fruit Topping

Using fresh fruit instead of canned fruit for the topping saves carbohydrates and calories.

FRENCH TOAST

- 1½ cups cholesterol-free egg substitute
- 2 teaspoons canola oil, divided
- 8 slices Italian multigrain or whole wheat bread

SWEET BUTTER SPREAD

- ¼ cup reduced-fat margarine
- 2 teaspoons sugar substitute*
- 2 teaspoons grated orange peel
- 1 teaspoon ground cinnamon
- 1 teaspoon vanilla

FRUIT TOPPING

- 1½ cups strawberries, hulled and quartered
- 1 cup sliced bananas
- ¼ cup orange juice
- 1 tablespoon sugar substitute*

*This recipe was tested using sucralose-based sugar substitute.

1. Preheat oven to 200°F. Pour egg substitute into shallow pie plate; set aside.

2. Heat 1 teaspoon oil in large nonstick skillet. Dip 4 slices bread into egg substitute coating both sides. Cook each side until golden brown (about 4 minutes). Transfer to plate and place in oven to keep warm. Repeat with remaining bread.

3. To make Sweet Butter Spread, combine margarine, 2 teaspoons sugar substitute, grated orange peel, cinnamon and vanilla in small bowl. Stir until well blended; set aside.

4. To make Fruit Topping, combine strawberries, bananas, orange juice and 1 tablespoon sugar substitute in medium bowl. Toss gently, yet thoroughly, to coat; set aside. To serve, spread each piece of French toast with about 1½ teaspoons Sweet Butter Spread and ¼ cup Fruit Topping.

MAKES 4 SERVINGS
(2 SLICES PER SERVING)

Calories: 337, Total Fat: 10 g, Saturated Fat: 1 g, Protein: 18 g, Carbohydrate: 48 g, Cholesterol: 0 mg, Fiber: 10 g, Sodium: 501 mg

Dietary Exchanges: 1 Fat, 3 Meat

Pumpkin Pancakes

Canned pumpkin adds potassium, vitamin A, and iron
to this recipe and has very few calories and carbohydrates.

1 cup all-purpose flour

3 tablespoons sugar substitute*

1 teaspoon baking powder

½ teaspoon pumpkin pie spice

¼ teaspoon baking soda

¼ teaspoon salt

¾ cup low-fat (1%) buttermilk

½ cup canned solid-pack pumpkin

1 egg

1 tablespoon canola oil

½ teaspoon vanilla

8 tablespoons sugar-free syrup

This recipe was tested using sucralose-based sugar substitute.

1. Combine flour, sugar substitute, baking powder, pumpkin pie spice, baking soda and salt in medium bowl; mix well.

2. Whisk together buttermilk, pumpkin, egg, oil and vanilla in small bowl. Add buttermilk mixture to flour mixture; stir until moist batter forms.

3. Spray griddle or large skillet with nonstick cooking spray; heat over medium-high heat. Spoon 2 tablespoons batter onto griddle for each pancake; spread batter to 3-inch diameter. Cook 2 to 3 minutes or until bubbles form on surface. Turn and cook about 1 minute more or until bottom is lightly browned. Serve with syrup.

MAKES 8 SERVINGS
(2 PANCAKES WITH 1 TABLESPOON SYRUP PER SERVING)

Calories: 108
Total Fat: 3 g
Saturated Fat: <1 g
Protein: 3 g
Carbohydrate: 18 g
Cholesterol: 27 mg
Fiber: 1 g
Sodium: 221 mg

Dietary Exchanges:
½ Fat, 1 Starch

Scrambled Eggs with Smoked Salmon

Replacing regular cream cheese with reduced-fat cream cheese is a healthy swap in this low-fat dish.

1 container (16 ounces) cholesterol-free egg substitute

⅛ teaspoon black pepper

2 tablespoons sliced green onions, with tops

1 ounce chilled reduced-fat cream cheese, cut into ¼-inch cubes

2 ounces smoked salmon, flaked

1. Whisk egg substitute and pepper in large bowl. Coat skillet with nonstick cooking spray; heat over medium heat. Pour egg substitute into skillet and stir. Cook 5 to 7 minutes or until mixture begins to set; stir occasionally while scraping bottom of pan.

2. Gently fold in onions, cream cheese and salmon. Cook and stir just until eggs are cooked through but still slightly moist, about 3 minutes.

MAKES 4 SERVINGS

Calories: 100, Total Fat: 3 g, Saturated Fat: 1 g, Protein: 15 g, Carbohydrate: 2 g, Cholesterol: 10 mg, Fiber: 0 g, Sodium: 560 mg

Dietary Exchanges: 2 Meat

Greek Isles Omelet

Instead of cooking the omelet in oil or butter, cooking spray is used to cut down on fat and calories.

¼ cup chopped onion

¼ cup canned artichoke hearts, rinsed and drained

¼ cup torn stemmed spinach leaves

¼ cup chopped plum tomato

2 tablespoons sliced pitted black olives, rinsed and drained

1 cup cholesterol-free egg substitute

Dash black pepper

MAKES 2 SERVINGS

Calories: 111
Total Fat: 3 g
Saturated Fat: <1 g
Protein: 13 g
Carbohydrate: 7 g
Cholesterol: 0 mg
Fiber: 1 g
Sodium: 538 mg

Dietary Exchanges:
2 Meat, 1 Vegetable

1. Coat small skillet with nonstick cooking spray; heat over medium heat. Add onion; cook and stir 2 minutes or until crisp-tender.

2. Add artichokes; cook and stir until heated through. Add spinach, tomato and olives; toss briefly. Remove from heat. Transfer vegetables to small bowl. Wipe out skillet and spray with cooking spray.

3. Combine egg substitute and pepper in medium bowl. Heat skillet over medium heat. Pour egg mixture into skillet. Cook over medium heat 5 to 7 minutes; as eggs begin to set, gently lift edge of omelet with spatula and tilt skillet so uncooked portion flows underneath.

4. When egg mixture is set, spoon vegetable mixture over half of omelet. Loosen omelet with spatula and fold in half. Slide omelet onto serving plate.

Spicy Mexican Frittata

Jalapeños pack plenty of flavor without adding many calories, carbohydrates, or fat.

1 jalapeño pepper*

1 clove garlic

1 medium tomato, peeled, halved, quartered and seeded

½ teaspoon ground coriander

½ teaspoon chili powder

½ cup chopped onion

1 cup frozen corn

6 egg whites

2 eggs

¼ cup fat-free (skim) milk

¼ teaspoon salt

¼ teaspoon black pepper

¼ cup (1 ounce) shredded part-skim farmer or mozzarella cheese

*Jalapeño peppers can sting and irritate the skin, so wear rubber gloves when handling peppers and do not touch your eyes.

1. Place jalapeño pepper and garlic in food processor or blender. Cover; process until finely chopped. Add tomato, coriander and chili powder. Cover; process until tomato is almost smooth.

2. Coat large skillet with nonstick cooking spray; heat over medium heat. Cook and stir onion until tender. Stir in tomato mixture and corn; cook 3 to 4 minutes or until liquid is almost evaporated, stirring occasionally.

3. Combine egg whites, eggs, milk, salt and black pepper in medium bowl. Add egg mixture all at once to skillet. Cook, without stirring, 2 minutes or until eggs begin to set. Run large spoon around edge of skillet, lifting eggs for even cooking. Remove skillet from heat when eggs are almost set but surface is still moist.

4. Sprinkle with cheese. Cover; let stand 3 to 4 minutes or until surface is set and cheese is melted. Cut into 4 wedges.

MAKES 4 SERVINGS

Calories: 129, Total Fat: 3 g, Saturated Fat: 1 g, Protein: 12 g, Carbohydrate: 14 g, Cholesterol: 108 mg, Fiber: 2 g, Sodium: 371 mg

Dietary Exchanges: 1 Meat, ½ Starch, 1 Vegetable

Light-Style Breakfast Sandwiches

Canadian bacon tastes like ham and has less fat than regular bacon.

4 egg whites

1 egg

¼ teaspoon salt (optional)

¼ teaspoon black pepper or ⅛ teaspoon hot pepper sauce

3 slices (2 ounces) Canadian bacon, chopped

1 green onion, thinly sliced

2 teaspoons butter

⅓ cup shredded reduced-fat sharp Cheddar cheese

4 multigrain or whole wheat English muffins, split and toasted

1. Beat egg whites, egg, salt, if desired, and pepper in medium bowl. Stir in Canadian bacon and green onion.

2. Heat butter in medium nonstick skillet over medium-high heat. Add egg mixture; cook, stirring frequently, 2 to 3 minutes or until eggs are just set. Remove from heat; stir in cheese. Serve on English muffins.

MAKES 4 SERVINGS
(1 SANDWICH PER SERVING)

Calories: 212
Total Fat: 7 g
Saturated Fat: 3 g
Protein: 16 g
Carbohydrate: 25 g
Cholesterol: 72 mg
Fiber: 3 g
Sodium: 536 mg

Dietary Exchanges:
1½ Meat, 2 Starch

Veggie-Beef Hash

This recipe is much lower in cholesterol and higher in fiber than most hash dishes, thanks to cholesterol-free egg whites and fresh vegetables.

4 ounces cooked roast beef, trimmed, finely chopped

1½ cups frozen seasoning blend*

1 cup shredded potatoes

½ cup shredded carrots

1 egg white or 2 tablespoons cholesterol-free egg substitute

½ teaspoon dried rosemary

½ teaspoon black pepper

½ cup reduced-sodium salsa (optional)

*Frozen seasoning blend is a combination of finely chopped onions, celery, green and red bell peppers, and parsley flakes. Frozen or fresh sliced bell peppers and onion can be substituted.

1. Combine beef, seasoning blend, potatoes, carrots, egg white, rosemary and pepper in large bowl.

2. Lightly spray large skillet with nonstick cooking spray; heat over medium-high heat. Add beef mixture; press down firmly to form large cake. Cook 4 minutes or until browned on bottom, pressing down on cake several times. Turn. Cook additional 4 minutes or until lightly browned and heated through. Serve with salsa, if desired.

MAKES 2 SERVINGS

Calories: 297
Total Fat: 9 g
Saturated Fat: 2 g
Protein: 22 g
Carbohydrate: 33 g
Cholesterol: 29 mg
Fiber: 5 g
Sodium: 378 mg

Dietary Exchanges:
1 Fat, 2 Meat, 2 Starch

Apple Cinnamon Grill

Using low-sugar preserves saves carbohydrates and calories in this effortless recipe.

4 teaspoons vegetable oil and yogurt spread

8 slices whole-grain cinnamon raisin bread

¼ cup reduced-fat cream cheese

¼ cup low-sugar red raspberry preserves

⅛ teaspoon ground cinnamon

1 medium Granny Smith apple (about 5 ounces), thinly sliced

**MAKES
4 SERVINGS**
(1 SANDWICH PER SERVING)

Calories: 265
Total Fat: 8 g
Saturated Fat: 3 g
Protein: 8 g
Carbohydrate: 36 g
Cholesterol: 10 mg
Fiber: 3 g
Sodium: 300 mg

Dietary Exchanges:
1 Fat, 2½ Starch

1. Spread ½ teaspoon vegetable oil and yogurt spread onto one side of each bread slice. On opposite side of 4 slices, spread 1 tablespoon cream cheese. Spread 1 tablespoon preserves on opposite side of remaining bread slices; sprinkle with cinnamon. Divide and layer apple slices on cream cheese side of 4 bread slices. Top each with each remaining bread slices.

2. Coat large skillet with nonstick cooking spray; heat over medium heat. Grill sandwiches 2 to 3 minutes on each side or until golden brown.

Potato Latke Sandwiches

Baking the latkes instead of frying them helps to make this a low-fat dish.

4 cups refrigerated or frozen shredded hash brown potatoes, thawed

¾ cup cholesterol-free egg substitute

1 teaspoon black pepper

Nonstick cooking spray

¼ cup (2 ounces) fat-free cream cheese

¼ cup chopped green onions

3 tablespoons imitation bacon bits

4 tablespoons unsweetened applesauce

1. Preheat oven to 425°F. Spray baking sheet with nonstick cooking spray; set aside.

2. Mix potatoes, egg substitute and pepper in medium bowl. Shape mixture into 8 patties (½ cup each); place on prepared baking sheet.

3. Bake 15 minutes. Remove from oven. Spray patties with cooking spray. Flip patties. Bake 6 minutes. Let stand 5 minutes.

4. Blend cream cheese, onions and bacon bits in small bowl. Spread 4 patties with 1 tablespoon cream cheese mixture and 1 tablespoon applesauce; top with remaining potato patties.

MAKES 4 SERVINGS

Calories: 247
Total Fat: 3 g
Saturated Fat: <1 g
Protein: 14 g
Carbohydrate: 42 g
Cholesterol: 6 mg
Fiber: 4 g
Sodium: 370 mg

Dietary Exchanges:
1 Meat, 2½ Starch

Pea and Spinach Frittata

Cooked brown rice adds fiber and vitamins to this frittata.

1 cup chopped onion

¼ cup water

1 cup frozen peas

1 cup torn stemmed
    spinach leaves

6 egg whites

2 eggs

½ cup cooked brown rice

¼ cup fat-free (skim) milk

2 tablespoons grated
    Romano or Parmesan
    cheese, plus additional
    for garnish (optional)

1 tablespoon chopped
    fresh mint or
    1 teaspoon dried mint
    leaves, crushed

¼ teaspoon black pepper

⅛ teaspoon salt

1. Coat large skillet with nonstick cooking spray. Combine onion and water in skillet. Bring to a boil over high heat. Reduce heat to medium. Cover; cook 2 to 3 minutes or until onion is tender. Stir in peas. Cook until peas are heated through; drain. Stir in spinach. Cook and stir about 1 minute or until spinach just starts to wilt.

2. Meanwhile, combine egg whites, eggs, rice, milk, Romano cheese, mint, pepper and salt in medium bowl. Add egg mixture to skillet. Cook, without stirring, 2 minutes until eggs begin to set. Run large spoon around edge of skillet, lifting eggs for even cooking. Remove skillet from heat when eggs are almost set but surface is still moist.

3. Cover; let stand 3 to 4 minutes or until surface is set. Garnish top with additional grated Romano or Parmesan cheese, if desired. Cut into 4 wedges to serve.

MAKES 4 SERVINGS

Calories: 162, Total Fat: 4 g, Saturated Fat: 1 g, Protein: 14 g, Carbohydrate: 18 g, Cholesterol: 110 mg, Fiber: 4 g, Sodium: 246 mg

Dietary Exchanges: 1 Meat, 1 Starch, 1½ Vegetable

Ham and Vegetable Omelet CARB

Lean ham and egg substitute make this omelet low in saturated fat and cholesterol.

2 ounces (about ½ cup) diced 95% fat-free ham

1 small onion, diced

½ medium green bell pepper, diced

½ medium red bell pepper, diced

2 cloves garlic, minced

1½ cups cholesterol-free egg substitute

⅛ teaspoon black pepper

½ cup (2 ounces) shredded reduced-fat Colby cheese, divided

1 medium tomato, chopped

Hot pepper sauce (optional)

MAKES 4 SERVINGS

Calories: 126
Total Fat: 4 g
Saturated Fat: 2 g
Protein: 16 g
Carbohydrate: 8 g
Cholesterol: 17 mg
Fiber: 1 g
Sodium: 443 mg

Dietary Exchanges:
2 Meat, 1 Vegetable

1. Coat 12-inch skillet with nonstick cooking spray; heat over medium-high heat. Add ham, onion, bell peppers and garlic; cook and stir 5 minutes or until vegetables are crisp-tender. Transfer mixture to large bowl; set aside.

2. Wipe out skillet with paper towels; coat with cooking spray. Heat over medium-high heat. Pour egg substitute into skillet; sprinkle with black pepper. Cook about 2 minutes or until bottom is set, lifting edge of egg with spatula to allow uncooked portion to flow underneath. Reduce heat to medium-low. Cover; cook 4 minutes or until top is set.

3. Gently slide omelet onto large serving plate; spoon ham mixture down center. Sprinkle with ¼ cup cheese. Carefully fold 2 sides of omelet over ham mixture. Sprinkle with remaining ¼ cup cheese and tomato. Cut into 4 wedges; serve immediately with hot pepper sauce, if desired.

Whole-Grain French Toast

Using whole wheat bread in place of white bread adds fiber and whole grains.

- ½ cup cholesterol-free egg substitute or 2 egg whites
- ¼ cup low-fat (1%) milk
- ½ teaspoon ground cinnamon
- ¼ teaspoon ground nutmeg
- 4 teaspoons butter, divided
- 8 slices 100% whole wheat bread or multigrain bread
- ⅓ cup pure maple syrup
- 1 cup fresh blueberries
- 2 teaspoons powdered sugar

**MAKES
4 SERVINGS**

(2 SLICES
FRENCH TOAST AND
¼ CUP BLUEBERRY
MIXTURE PER
SERVING)

Calories: 251
Total Fat: 6 g
Saturated Fat: 3 g
Protein: 12 g
Carbohydrate: 46 g
Cholesterol: 11 mg
Fiber: 5 g
Sodium: 324 mg

Dietary Exchanges:
1 Fruit, 1 Meat, 2 Starch

1. Heat oven to 400°F. Coat baking sheet with nonstick cooking spray; set aside.

2. Combine egg substitute, milk, cinnamon and nutmeg in pie plate or shallow bowl; mix well.

3. Melt 1 teaspoon butter in large nonstick skillet over medium heat. Quickly dip each bread slice in milk mixture to lightly coat on both sides; let excess mixture drip back into plate. Cook 2 slices at a time in skillet until golden brown, about 2 minutes per side. Transfer French toast to baking sheet. Repeat with remaining butter, bread and milk mixture. Bake 5 to 6 minutes or until heated through.

4. Pour syrup into small microwave-safe bowl. Microwave, uncovered, on HIGH 30 seconds or until bubbly. Stir In blueberries. Transfer French toast to 4 serving plates; top evenly with blueberry mixture. Place powdered sugar in wire strainer; shake over blueberries.

Very Berry Yogurt Parfaits

Fat-free yogurt and sliced almonds save almost half the fat and calories of a typical yogurt parfait.

3 cups plain fat-free yogurt

2 tablespoons sugar-free berry preserves

1 packet sugar substitute*

½ teaspoon vanilla

2 cups sliced fresh strawberries

1 cup fresh blueberries

4 tablespoons toasted sliced almonds

This recipe was tested using sucralose-based sugar substitute.

1. Combine yogurt, preserves, sugar substitute and vanilla in medium bowl.

2. Layer ½ cup yogurt mixture, ¼ cup strawberries, ¼ cup blueberries and ¼ cup yogurt mixture in each of 4 dessert dishes. Top each parfait with remaining ¼ cup strawberries and 1 tablespoon almonds. Serve immediately.

Tip: Try another flavor of sugar-free preserves for a simple variation.

MAKES 4 SERVINGS

Calories: 179
Total Fat: 3 g
Saturated Fat: <1 g
Protein: 10 g
Carbohydrate: 33 g
Cholesterol: 4 mg
Fiber: 3 g
Sodium: 104 mg

Dietary Exchanges:
1½ Fruit, 1 Milk

Sausage and Cheddar Omelet

Turkey sausage replaces regular sausage for less saturated fat.

2 uncooked turkey breakfast sausage links (about 1 ounce each)

1 small onion, diced

1½ cups cholesterol-free egg substitute

⅛ teaspoon salt

¼ teaspoon black pepper

½ cup (2 ounces) shredded reduced-fat Cheddar cheese, divided

Sliced green onions (optional)

1. Coat 12-inch skillet with nonstick cooking spray and heat over medium-high heat. Remove sausage from casings. Add sausage and diced onion to skillet. Cook about 5 minutes or until sausage is no longer pink and onion is crisp-tender, stirring to break up meat. Remove from skillet.

2. Wipe out skillet with paper towels; coat with nonstick cooking spray. Heat over medium-high heat. Pour egg substitute into skillet; sprinkle with salt and pepper. Cook 2 minutes or until bottom is set, lifting edge of egg to allow uncooked portion to flow underneath. Reduce heat to medium-low. Cover; cook 4 minutes or until top is set.

3. Gently slide cooked egg onto large serving plate; spoon sausage mixture down center. Sprinkle with ¼ cup cheese. Fold sides of omelet over sausage mixture. Sprinkle with remaining ¼ cup cheese and garnish with green onions, if desired. Cut into 4 pieces; serve immediately.

MAKES 4 SERVINGS

Calories: 133
Total Fat: 6 g
Saturated Fat: 3 g
Protein: 15 g
Carbohydrate: 4 g
Cholesterol: 19 mg
Fiber: <1 g
Sodium: 523 mg

Dietary Exchanges:
2 Meat, 1 Vegetable

Mexican Breakfast Burrito 🌾

Low-fat fillings like black beans and egg substitute make this a hearty burrito without all the calories.

1 container (16 ounces) cholesterol-free egg substitute

⅛ teaspoon black pepper

⅓ cup drained black beans

2 tablespoons sliced green onions

2 (10-inch) flour tortillas

3 tablespoons shredded reduced-fat Cheddar cheese

3 tablespoons salsa

1. Whisk egg substitute and pepper in large bowl. Coat large skillet with nonstick cooking spray; heat over medium heat. Pour egg substitute into skillet and stir. Cook 5 to 7 minutes or until mixture begins to set; stir occasionally while scraping bottom of pan. Lightly fold in beans and onions. Cook and stir just until egg substitute is cooked through but still slightly moist, about 3 minutes.

2. Spoon mixture down centers of tortillas; top with cheese. Fold in opposite sides of each tortilla; roll up burrito-style and top with salsa. Cut in half.

MAKES 4 SERVINGS
(½ BURRITO PER SERVING)

Calories: 200, Total Fat: 4 g, Saturated Fat: 1 g, Protein: 17 g, Carbohydrates: 22 g, Cholesterol: 5 mg, Dietary Fiber: 5 g, Sodium: 590 mg

Dietary Exchanges: 1½ Meat, 1½ Starch

Family Favorites

All-in-One Burger Stew

A few simple and low-fat ingredients like lean ground beef and vegetables make this a healthy and well-rounded dish.

1 pound lean ground beef

2 cups frozen Italian-style vegetables

1 can (about 14 ounces) diced tomatoes with basil and garlic

1 can (about 14 ounces) beef broth

2½ cups uncooked medium egg noodles

Salt and black pepper (optional)

1. Brown beef in Dutch oven or large skillet over medium-high heat 6 to 8 minutes, stirring to break up meat. Drain fat.

2. Add vegetables, tomatoes and broth; bring to a boil over high heat.

3. Add noodles; reduce heat to medium. Cover; cook 12 to 15 minutes or until noodles and vegetables are tender. Season with salt and pepper, if desired.

Tip: To complete this meal, serve with a simple salad, if desired.

MAKES 6 SERVINGS

Calories: 260, Total Fat: 11 g, Saturated Fat: 4 g, Protein: 17 g, Carbohydrate: 20 g, Cholesterol: 62 mg, Fiber: 2 g, Sodium: 428 mg

Dietary Exchanges: 1 Fat, 1 Starch, 1 Vegetable

Lemon Chicken ▼CARB

Boneless skinless chicken is an ideal lean protein source and has no carbohydrates and very little fat.

2 tablespoons extra-virgin olive oil, divided

4 boneless skinless chicken breasts (4 ounces each) flattened to ½ inch thickness

½ cup white wine

Juice of 1 fresh lemon

1 cup chopped fresh mushrooms, sliced

2 tablespoons capers

1 teaspoon fresh dill, plus additional for garnish

Lemon wedges (optional)

1. Heat 1 teaspoon oil in large nonstick skillet over medium-high heat. Tilt skillet to coat bottom lightly and cook chicken 3 to 4 minutes or until beginning to lightly brown.

2. Meanwhile, combine remaining ingredients except oil in small bowl; stir to blend.

3. Turn chicken pieces, pour wine mixture evenly over chicken. Reduce heat, cover tightly and simmer 8 minutes or until chicken is no longer pink in center.

4. Remove chicken from skillet and place on serving platter. Increase heat to medium-high and boil 1 minute to reduce wine mixture slightly. Remove from heat, stir in remaining oil and spoon evenly over all. Garnish with additional dill and fresh lemon wedges, if desired.

MAKES 4 SERVINGS

Calories: 221
Total Fat: 10 g
Saturated Fat: 2 g
Protein: 25 g
Carbohydrate: 3 g
Cholesterol: 72 mg
Dietary Fiber: <1 g
Sodium: 236 mg

Dietary Exchanges:
3 Meat, 1 Vegetable

Quick Chicken Sausage Jambalaya

Using chicken sausage instead of pork sausage
saves fat, cholesterol, and calories.

1 pouch (about 9 ounces)
   ready-to-serve brown
   rice

2 teaspoons canola oil

1 cup chopped onion

1 small green bell pepper,
   diced

3 cloves garlic, minced

2 tablespoons all-purpose
   flour

1 can (about 14 ounces)
   diced fire-roasted
   tomatoes, undrained

1 cup reduced-sodium
   chicken broth

1 package (9 ounces) fully
   cooked andouille or
   spicy chicken sausage,
   cut into ½-inch-thick
   slices

1 teaspoon dried thyme

¼ teaspoon hot pepper
   sauce or smoked
   hot pepper sauce
   (optional)

   Red chiles (optional)

1. Cook rice according to package directions, omitting any salt or fat.

2. Heat oil in large saucepan over medium heat. Add onion, bell pepper and garlic; cook 5 minutes, stirring occasionally. Stir in flour; cook and stir 1 minute. Add tomatoes with their juices, broth, sausage, thyme and hot pepper sauce, if desired. Bring to a boil over high heat. Reduce heat; simmer uncovered 15 minutes or until vegetables are tender and sauce thickens. Stir in rice or serve over rice. Garnish with red chiles, if desired.

Note: Jambalaya is a Louisiana Creole dish with French and Spanish influences.

MAKES 4 SERVINGS
(½ CUP RICE AND 1 CUP JAMBALAYA PER SERVING)

Calories: 291, Total Fat: 7 g, Saturated Fat: 1 g, Protein: 19 g, Carbohydrate: 38 g, Cholesterol: 54 mg, Fiber: 4 g, Sodium: 511 mg

Dietary Exchanges: 2 Meat, 2 Starch, 1 Vegetable

Grilled Flank Steak with Horseradish Sauce

Flank steak is one of the leaner cuts of beef and is topped with fat-free horseradish sauce.

1 beef flank steak (about 1 pound)

2 tablespoons reduced-sodium soy sauce

1 tablespoon red wine vinegar

2 cloves garlic, minced

½ teaspoon black pepper

1 cup fat-free sour cream

¼ cup finely chopped fresh parsley

1 tablespoon prepared horseradish

1 tablespoon Dijon mustard

½ teaspoon salt

6 sourdough rolls, split

6 romaine lettuce leaves

1. Place flank steak in large resealable food storage bag. Add soy sauce, vinegar, garlic and pepper. Seal bag; turn to coat. Marinate in refrigerator at least 1 hour.

2. Prepare grill for direct cooking. Drain steak; discard marinade. Grill steak over medium heat, uncovered, 17 to 21 minutes for medium-rare to medium or until desired doneness, turning once. Cover with foil; let stand 15 minutes. Thinly slice steak across the grain.

3. Combine sour cream, parsley, horseradish, mustard and salt in small bowl until well blended. Spread rolls with horseradish sauce; layer with lettuce and sliced steak.

MAKES 6 SERVINGS
(1 ROLL WITH 2 OUNCES COOKED BEEF, 3 TABLESPOONS PLUS 1 TEASPOON HORSERADISH SAUCE AND 1 LETTUCE LEAF PER SERVING)

Calories: 307, Total Fat: 9 g, Saturated Fat: 3 g, Protein: 24 g, Carbohydrate: 29 g, Cholesterol: 52 mg, Fiber: 1 g, Sodium: 600 mg

Dietary Exchanges: 3 Meat, 2 Starch

Easy Cheesy Ham and Veggie Rice Casserole

Lean ham significantly reduces the calories, fat, and sodium in this casserole.

1 bag (3½ ounces) boil-in-bag brown rice

2 cups broccoli florets

1 cup (3 ounces) matchstick-size carrot pieces

6 ounces lean, reduced-sodium ham, diced

2 ounces Swiss cheese, broken into small pieces

3 ounces reduced-fat shredded sharp Cheddar cheese, divided

1 tablespoon reduced-fat margarine

⅛ teaspoon ground red pepper

1. Cook rice in large saucepan according to package directions, omitting any salt or fat. Remove rice packet when cooked; reserve water.

2. Add broccoli and carrots to water in saucepan, bring to a boil, reduce heat, cover and simmer 3 minutes or until broccoli is crisp-tender.

3. Drain vegetables and return to saucepan. Stir in rice. Heat over medium-low heat. Add ham, Swiss cheese, 1 ounce Cheddar, margarine and red pepper; stir gently. Sprinkle evenly with remaining Cheddar; cover and cook 3 minutes or until cheese melts.

MAKES 4 SERVINGS
(1½ CUPS PER SERVING)

Calories: 283
Total Fat: 12 g
Saturated Fat: 6 g
Protein: 19 g
Carbohydrate: 26 g
Cholesterol: 48 mg
Fiber: 2 g
Sodium: 616 mg

Dietary Exchanges:
1 Fat, 2 Meat, 1 Starch, 1 Vegetable

Barbecued Shrimp over Tropical Rice

Shrimp are high in protein and low in fat and calories to make this a healthy and fit recipe.

20 frozen large raw shrimp, peeled and deveined (26 to 30 per pound)

½ cup uncooked brown rice

½ cup barbecue sauce

2 teaspoons fresh grated ginger

1 cup chopped fresh mango* (about 1 medium mango)

2 tablespoons finely chopped red onion

1 tablespoon chopped fresh cilantro

1 tablespoon finely chopped and seeded jalapeño pepper**

2 teaspoons lime juice

*To chop a mango, first cut off all four sides around the pit. Then slide a knife between the skin and meat of the mango. Remove skin and cut into chunks then chop into smaller pieces.

**Jalapeño peppers can sting and irritate the skin, so wear rubber gloves when handling peppers and do not touch your eyes.

1. Thaw shrimp according to package directions.

2. Cook brown rice according to package directions, omitting any salt or fat; set aside.

3. Meanwhile, thread shrimp onto 4 wooden skewers, leaving ⅛-inch space between shrimp. Stir together barbecue sauce and ginger in small bowl. Grill shrimp on greased rack of uncovered grill directly over medium heat for 6 to 7 minutes or until shrimp are opaque, turning once and brushing frequently with sauce mixture.

4. Stir mango, onion, cilantro, jalapeño and lime juice into hot rice. Spoon onto serving plates. Serve shrimp on top of rice mixture.

Note: Mangos are chock-full of vitamins A and C. They also are rich in fiber and contain more than 20 different vitamins and minerals.

Tip: Soak wooden skewers in water 20 minutes before using to prevent scorching.

MAKES 4 SERVINGS
(½ CUP RICE AND 5 SHRIMP PER SERVING)

Calories: 200, Total Fat: 2 g, Saturated Fat: <1 g, Protein: 9 g, Carbohydrate: 37 g, Cholesterol: 53 mg, Fiber: 2 g, Sodium: 396 mg

Dietary Exchanges: 1 Meat, 2 Starch

Turkey Stroganoff

This is a tasty version of a traditional recipe without the fat–thanks to fat-free sour cream and lean turkey.

2 cups sliced mushrooms

1 stalk celery, thinly sliced

1 medium shallot or ¼ small onion, minced

½ cup reduced-sodium chicken broth

¼ teaspoon dried thyme

⅛ teaspoon black pepper

1 turkey tenderloin, turkey breast or boneless skinless chicken thighs (about 5 ounces each), cut into bite-size chunks

2 teaspoons all-purpose flour

¼ cup fat-free sour cream

⅛ teaspoon salt (optional)

⅔ cup cooked wide cholesterol-free whole wheat egg noodles

1. Coat large skillet with nonstick cooking spray. Add mushrooms, celery and shallot. Cook over medium heat, stirring frequently, 5 minutes or until mushrooms and shallot are tender. Spoon into small slow cooker. Add chicken broth, thyme and pepper; stir. Add turkey. Cover; cook on LOW 5 to 6 hours.

2. Combine flour and sour cream in small bowl. Spoon 2 tablespoons liquid from slow cooker into bowl; stir well. Stir sour cream mixture into slow cooker. Cover; cook 10 minutes more. Stir in salt, if desired.

3. Spoon ⅓ cup cooked noodles onto each of 2 plates to serve. Top each with half of turkey mixture.

MAKES 2 SERVINGS
(1 CUP TURKEY MIXTURE PLUS ⅓ CUP NOODLES PER SERVING)

Calories: 310, Total Fat: 3 g, Saturated Fat: 1 g, Protein: 30 g, Carbohydrate: 41 g, Cholesterol: 100 mg, Fiber: 3 g, Sodium: 123 mg

Dietary Exchanges: 3 Meat, 2 Starch

Prosciutto-Wrapped Chicken with Goat Cheese CRB

Prosciutto is a leaner alternative to bacon with less carbohydrates, calories, fat, and sodium.

8 slices lean prosciutto

4 boneless skinless chicken breasts (4 ounces each) pounded to ¼ inch thickness and cut in half crosswise

2 to 3 ounces goat cheese

16 to 24 basil leaves, plus additional for garnish

1 teaspoon olive oil

1 shallot, finely chopped

2 tablespoons dry red wine

1. Preheat oven to 350°F. Coat an 8×8-inch pan with nonstick cooking spray.

2. Lay out prosciutto on clean work surface or cutting board. Place chicken on top of each prosciutto piece. Top chicken with goat cheese. Place 3 basil leaves on top of each mound of cheese. Wrap prosciutto around chicken and secure with toothpicks in an X fashion.

3. Heat oil in small skillet over medium heat. Add shallot and cook and stir about 2 minutes, until softened. Deglaze pan with wine. Pour shallot and wine over chicken and bake 20 minutes in prepared pan. Remove from oven and garnish with fresh basil, if desired.

MAKES 4 SERVINGS

Calories: 219, Total Fat: 8 g, Saturated Fat: 3 g, Protein: 31 g, Carbohydrate: 1 g, Cholesterol: 92 mg, Dietary Fiber: 0 mg, Sodium: 643 mg

Dietary Exchanges: 4 Meat

Tuna Noodle Casserole

Replacing regular cream of mushroom soup with reduced-fat cream of mushroom soup cuts out half the fat.

8 ounces wide cholesterol-free whole wheat egg noodles

½ cup finely chopped onion

1 can (10 ounces) reduced-fat condensed cream of mushroom soup, undiluted

½ cup reduced-fat sour cream

½ cup low-fat (1%) milk

⅛ teaspoon ground red pepper

12 ounces tuna packed in water, drained and broken into chunks

1½ cups frozen baby peas

1 slice whole wheat or multigrain bread

½ teaspoon paprika

Nonstick cooking spray

1. Preheat oven to 350°F. Spray 2½-quart casserole with nonstick cooking spray; set aside. Cook noodles in large saucepan according to package directions, omitting any salt or fat. Drain; return to saucepan.

2. Meanwhile, coat large skillet with nonstick cooking spray. Add onion; cook over medium heat 4 to 5 minutes or until tender. Stir in soup, sour cream, milk and red pepper until well blended. Remove from heat. Add soup mixture, tuna and peas to noodles. Toss well; transfer mixture to prepared casserole.

3. Tear bread into pieces; place in bowl of food processor. Process until finely minced. Sprinkle evenly over casserole; top with paprika. Spray top of casserole with cooking spray. Bake 30 to 35 minutes or until heated through.

MAKES 6 SERVINGS
(1¼ CUPS PER SERVING)

Calories: 315, Total Fat: 5 g, Saturated Fat: 2 g, Protein: 23 g, Carbohydrate: 41 g, Cholesterol: 31 mg, Fiber: 4 g, Sodium: 502 mg

Dietary Exchanges: 2 Meat, 3 Starch

Chili Beef and Corn Casserole

Fat-free sour cream and reduced-fat cheese are guiltless casserole toppings.

¾ **pound 95% lean ground beef**

¼ **cup reduced-sodium salsa**

2 **teaspoons chili powder**

1½ **teaspoons ground cumin**

2 **cups frozen corn, thawed**

2 **ounces chopped collard greens, about ½-inch pieces (1 cup packed)**

½ **cup fat-free sour cream**

¼ **cup (1 ounce) shredded reduced-fat sharp Cheddar cheese**

1. Preheat oven 350°F. Brown beef 6 to 8 minutes in large nonstick skillet over medium-high heat, stirring to break up meat. Drain fat. Add salsa, chili powder and cumin; cook and stir 1 minute. Remove from heat.

2. Coat 8-inch square baking pan with nonstick cooking spray. Combine corn and collard greens in prepared pan. Spoon beef mixture evenly over vegetables; cover with foil.

3. Bake 25 minutes or until greens are tender. Top each serving with 2 tablespoons sour cream and 1 tablespoon cheese.

**MAKES
4 SERVINGS**
(1 CUP PER SERVING)

Calories: 240
Total Fat: 5 g
Saturated Fat: 2 g
Protein: 25 g
Carbohydrate: 25 g
Cholesterol: 60 mg
Fiber: 3 g
Sodium: 249 mg

Dietary Exchanges:
3 Meat, 1½ Starch

Sloppy Joe Sliders

Lean ground beef makes this a satisfying meal without all the fat.

12 ounces 90% lean ground beef

1 can (about 14 ounces) stewed tomatoes with Mexican seasonings

½ cup frozen mixed vegetables, thawed

½ cup chopped green bell pepper

3 tablespoons ketchup

2 teaspoons Worcestershire sauce

1 teaspoon ground cumin

1 teaspoon cider vinegar

24 mini whole wheat rolls or 1-ounce rolls, split and warmed

1. Brown ground beef in a large nonstick skillet over medium-high heat, 6 to 8 minutes, stirring to break up meat.

2. Add tomatoes, mixed vegetables, bell pepper, ketchup, Worcestershire sauce, cumin and vinegar; bring to a boil. Reduce heat; cover and simmer 15 minutes or until peppers are tender and mixture has thickened. Break up large pieces of tomato. To serve, spoon 2 tablespoons into each bun.

MAKES 8 SERVINGS
(3 SLIDERS PER SERVING)

Calories: 324, Total Fat: 7 g, Saturated Fat: 2 g, Protein: 17 g, Carbohydrate: 50 g, Cholesterol: 23 mg, Fiber: 8 g, Sodium: 620 mg

Dietary Exchanges: ½ Fat, 3 Meat, 3 Starch, 1 Vegetable

Pork and Sweet Potato Skillet

Pork tenderloin is the leanest cut of pork and makes this a healthful main dish.

¾ pound pork tenderloin, cut into 1-inch cubes

1 tablespoon plus 1 teaspoon butter, divided

¼ teaspoon salt

⅛ teaspoon black pepper

2 medium sweet potatoes, peeled and cut into ½-inch pieces (about 2 cups)

1 small onion, sliced

¼ pound reduced-fat smoked turkey sausage, halved lengthwise and cut into ½-Inch pieces

1 small green or red apple, cored and cut into ½-inch pieces

½ cup prepared sweet-and-sour sauce

2 tablespoons chopped fresh parsley (optional)

1. Place pork and 1 teaspoon butter into large nonstick skillet; cook and stir 2 to 3 minutes over medium-high heat or until pork is no longer pink. Season with salt and pepper. Remove from skillet.

2. Add remaining 1 tablespoon butter, potatoes and onion to skillet. Cover; cook and stir over medium-low heat 8 to 10 minutes or until tender.

3. Add pork, sausage, apple and sweet-and-sour sauce to skillet; cook and stir until heated through. Garnish with parsley, if desired.

MAKES 4 SERVINGS
(1½ CUPS PER SERVING)

Calories: 309, Total Fat: 7 g, Saturated Fat: 4 g, Protein: 22 g, Carbohydrate: 39 g, Cholesterol: 71 mg, Fiber: 3 g, Sodium: 565 mg

Dietary Exchanges: 1 Fat, ½ Fruit, 3 Meat, 2 Starch, ½ Vegetable

Barley Beef Stroganoff

Adding barley to this recipe reduces the fat and increases the fiber.

2½ cups reduced-sodium vegetable broth or water

⅔ cup uncooked pearl barley (not quick-cooking)

1 package (6 ounces) sliced mushrooms

½ teaspoon dried marjoram

½ teaspoon black pepper

½ pound 95% lean ground beef

½ cup chopped celery

½ cup minced green onions

¼ cup fat-free half-and-half

Minced fresh parsley (optional)

MAKES 4 SERVINGS
(1¼ CUPS PER SERVING)

Calories: 287
Total Fat: 10 g
Saturated Fat: 4 g
Protein: 17 g
Carbohydrate: 34 g
Cholesterol: 41 mg
Fiber: 7 g
Sodium: 358 mg

Dietary Exchanges:
½ Fat, 2 Meat, 2 Starch

Slow Cooker Directions

1. Place broth, barley, mushrooms, marjoram and pepper in slow cooker. Cover; cook on LOW 6 to 7 hours.

2. Brown beef in large skillet over medium-high heat 6 to 8 minutes, stirring to break up meat. Drain fat. Add celery and green onions; cook and stir 3 minutes.

3. Stir beef mixture and half-and-half into slow cooker mixture. Cover; cook on HIGH 10 to 15 minutes or until beef is hot and vegetables are tender. Garnish with parsley, if desired.

Turkey Sliders

Lean ground turkey is a lower fat alternative to beef.

1 tablespoon Worcestershire sauce

2 tablespoons low-fat mayonnaise

⅛ teaspoon salt

¼ teaspoon black pepper

¼ cup finely chopped green onions

1 pound ground turkey breast

12 mini whole wheat pita breads

12 baby spinach leaves

¼ cup shredded reduced-fat sharp Cheddar cheese

1 shallot, thinly sliced into 12 slices

1 tablespoon steak sauce (optional)

1. Combine Worcestershire sauce, mayonnaise, salt and pepper in large bowl. Mix well. Add onions and turkey. Gently knead ingredients together. Do not overwork. Shape into 12 patties, about 2 inches across.

2. Coat large nonstick skillet with nonstick cooking spray and heat over medium heat. Arrange patties in skillet; do not crowd. Cook 5 to 6 minutes on first side or until lightly browned; turn over and cook second side about 4 to 5 minutes or until cooked through. Remove from skillet.

3. Split pita breads open and line 6 bread halves with 2 baby spinach leaves. Add 1 turkey patty and top with 1 teaspoon cheese, 1 shallot slice and ½ teaspoon steak sauce, if desired. Top with remaining pita bread slices.

Note: Ground turkey comes in various percentages of lean. Regular ground turkey (85% lean) is a combination of white and dark meat, which is comparable in fat to some lean cuts of ground beef. Ground turkey breast is lowest in fat (up to 99% lean), but it can dry out very easily when grilled. To keep the best texture, gently form patties or meatballs, and do not press down on burgers with a spatula as they grill.

MAKES 6 SERVINGS
(2 SLIDERS PER SERVING)

Calories: 262, Total Fat: 4 g, Saturated Fat: 1 g, Protein: 24 g, Carbohydrate: 31 g, Cholesterol: 43 mg, Fiber: 2 g, Sodium: 596 mg

Dietary Exchanges: 2 Meat, 2 Starch

Chicken Gumbo

Replacing chicken stock with fat-free, reduced-sodium chicken broth lightens up this recipe without sacrificing flavor.

2 tablespoons all-purpose flour

2 teaspoons blackened seasoning mix or Creole seasoning mix

¾ pound boneless skinless chicken thighs, cut into ¾-inch pieces

2 teaspoons olive oil

1 large onion, coarsely chopped

½ cup sliced celery

2 teaspoons minced garlic

1 can (about 14 ounces) fat-free reduced-sodium chicken broth

1 can (about 14 ounces) no-salt-added stewed tomatoes, undrained

1 large green bell pepper, cut into chunks

1 teaspoon filé powder (optional)

2 cups hot cooked rice

2 tablespoons chopped fresh parsley

1. Combine flour and blackened seasoning mix in large resealable food storage bag. Add chicken; seal bag. Toss to coat.

2. Heat oil in large deep nonstick skillet or saucepan over medium heat. Add chicken; sprinkle with any remaining flour mixture. Cook and stir 3 minutes. Add onion, celery and garlic; cook and stir 3 minutes.

3. Add broth, tomatoes with their juices and bell pepper; bring to a boil. Reduce heat; cover and simmer 20 minutes or until vegetables are tender. Uncover; simmer 5 to 10 minutes or until liquid is slightly reduced. Remove from heat; stir in filé powder, if desired. Ladle into shallow bowls; top with rice and parsley.

Note: Filé powder, made from dried sassafras leaves, thickens and adds flavor to gumbos. Look for it in the herb and spice section of your supermarket. Never add it to gumbo while it's still on the heat, or if you plan to reheat leftovers, because cooking filé powder causes it to become stringy and tough.

MAKES 4 SERVINGS
(1½ CUPS GUMBO WITH ½ CUP RICE PER SERVING)

Calories: 306, Total Fat: 9 g, Saturated Fat: 2 g, Protein: 18 g, Carbohydrate: 38 g, Cholesterol: 46 mg, Fiber: 3 g, Sodium: 302 mg

Dietary Exchanges: 1 Fat, 2 Meat, 2 Starch, 1 Vegetable

Chicken Pot Pie

Fat-free half-and-half and reduced-fat crescent rolls go a long way in cutting down fat and calories in this classic casserole.

½ cup plus 2 tablespoons fat-free reduced-sodium chicken broth, divided

2 teaspoons margarine

2 cups sliced mushrooms

1 cup diced red bell pepper

½ cup chopped onion

½ cup chopped celery

2 tablespoons all-purpose flour

½ cup fat-free half-and-half

2 cups cubed cooked chicken breasts (see Note)

1 teaspoon minced fresh dill

½ teaspoon salt

¼ teaspoon black pepper

2 reduced-fat refrigerated crescent rolls

1. Heat 2 tablespoons broth and margarine in medium saucepan over medium heat until margarine is melted. Add mushrooms, bell pepper, onion and celery; cook and stir 7 to 10 minutes or until vegetables are tender.

2. Stir in flour; cook 1 minute. Stir in remaining ½ cup broth; cook and stir until liquid thickens. Reduce heat and stir in half-and-half. Stir in chicken, dill, salt and black pepper.

3. Preheat oven to 375°F. Spray 1-quart casserole with nonstick cooking spray. Spoon chicken mixture into prepared casserole. Roll out crescent rolls and place over chicken mixture.*

4. Bake 20 minutes or until topping is golden and filling is bubbly.

Reserve remaining rolls for another use.

Note: For 2 cups cubed cooked chicken breast, gently simmer 3 small chicken breasts in 2 cups fat-free reduced-sodium chicken broth about 20 minutes or until meat is no longer pink in center. Cool and cut into cubes. Reserve chicken broth for pot pie, if desired.

MAKES 4 SERVINGS
(1 CUP PER SERVING)

Calories: 256, Total Fat: 8 g, Saturated Fat: 2 g, Protein: 24 g, Carbohydrate: 18 g, Cholesterol: 50 mg, Fiber: 2 g, Sodium: 541 mg

Dietary Exchanges: 3 Meat, 1 Starch, 1 Vegetable

Turkey Vegetable Chili Mac

Ground turkey adds protein and flavor without adding excessive fat.

¾ pound 93% lean ground turkey

½ cup chopped onion

2 cloves garlic, minced

1 can (about 15 ounces) black beans, rinsed and drained

1 can (about 14 ounces) Mexican-style stewed tomatoes, undrained

1 can (about 14 ounces) no-salt-added diced tomatoes, undrained

1 cup frozen corn

1 teaspoon Mexican seasoning

½ cup uncooked elbow macaroni

⅓ cup reduced-fat sour cream

1. Coat large saucepan or Dutch oven with nonstick cooking spray; heat over medium heat. Add turkey, onion and garlic; cook and stir 5 minutes or until turkey is no longer pink.

2. Stir beans, tomatoes with their juices, corn and Mexican seasoning into saucepan; bring to a boil over high heat. Cover; reduce heat to low. Simmer 15 minutes, stirring occasionally.

3. Meanwhile, cook pasta according to package directions, omitting any salt or fat. Rinse and drain pasta; stir into saucepan. Simmer, uncovered, 2 to 3 minutes or until heated through.

4. Top each serving with dollop of sour cream. Garnish as desired.

MAKES 6 SERVINGS
(1 CUP PER SERVING)

Calories: 236
Total Fat: 6 g
Saturated Fat: 1 g
Protein: 17 g
Carbohydrate: 34 g
Cholesterol: 25 mg
Fiber: 6 g
Sodium: 445 mg

Dietary Exchanges:
½ Fat, 1 Meat,
1½ Starch, 2 Vegetable

Enlightened Macaroni and Cheese

Typical macaroni and cheese is transformed by substituting whole milk with evaporated skim milk and by using pimientos in place of bacon.

8 ounces uncooked rotini pasta or elbow macaroni

1 tablespoon all-purpose flour

2 teaspoons cornstarch

¼ teaspoon dry mustard

1 can (12 ounces) evaporated skimmed milk

1 cup (4 ounces) shredded reduced-fat sharp Cheddar cheese

½ cup (2 ounces) shredded reduced-fat Monterey Jack cheese

1 jar (2 ounces) diced pimientos, drained and rinsed

1 teaspoon Worcestershire sauce

¼ teaspoon black pepper

1 tablespoon plain dry bread crumbs

1 tablespoon paprika

1. Preheat oven to 375°F. Cook pasta according to package directions, omitting any salt or fat. Drain and set aside.

2. Combine flour, cornstarch and mustard in medium saucepan; stir in evaporated milk until smooth. Cook and stir over low heat about 8 minutes or until slightly thickened.

3. Remove from heat; stir in cheeses, pimientos, Worcestershire sauce and pepper. Add pasta; mix well.

4. Spray 1½-quart casserole with nonstick cooking spray. Spoon mixture into casserole; sprinkle with bread crumbs and paprika.

5. Bake 20 minutes or until bubbly and heated through.

**MAKES
6 SERVINGS**
(1 CUP PER SERVING)

Calories: 266
Total Fat: 6 g
Saturated Fat: 3 g
Protein: 18 g
Carbohydrate: 35 g
Cholesterol: 18 mg
Fiber: 2 g
Sodium: 200 mg

Dietary Exchanges:
½ Fat, 1 Meat, ½ Milk,
2 Starch

Ravioli with Homemade Tomato Sauce

Fresh ingredients and low-fat cheeses replace heavy sauces and high-fat cheese to make this a healthy pasta plate.

3 cloves garlic, peeled

½ cup fresh basil leaves

3 tomatoes, peeled, seeded and quartered

2 tablespoons tomato paste

2 tablespoons prepared fat-free Italian salad dressing

1 tablespoon balsamic vinegar

¼ teaspoon black pepper

1 package (9 ounces) uncooked refrigerated reduced-fat cheese ravioli

2 cups shredded spinach leaves

1 cup (4 ounces) shredded part-skim mozzarella cheese

1. To prepare tomato sauce, process garlic in food processor until coarsely chopped. Add basil; process until coarsely chopped. Add tomatoes, tomato paste, salad dressing, vinegar and pepper; process, using on/off pulsing action, until tomatoes are chopped.

2. Spray 9-inch square microwavable dish with nonstick cooking spray. Spread 1 cup tomato sauce in dish. Layer half of ravioli and spinach over tomato sauce. Repeat layers with 1 cup tomato sauce and remaining ravioli and spinach. Top with remaining 1 cup tomato sauce. Cover with plastic wrap; refrigerate 1 to 8 hours.

3. Vent plastic wrap. Microwave on MEDIUM (50%) 20 minutes or until pasta is tender and hot. Sprinkle with cheese. Microwave on HIGH 3 minutes or just until cheese melts. Let stand, covered, 5 minutes before serving.

**MAKES
6 SERVINGS**

Calories: 206
Total Fat: 6 g
Saturated Fat: 3 g
Protein: 13 g
Carbohydrate: 26 g
Cholesterol: 40 mg
Fiber: 3 g
Sodium: 401 mg

Dietary Exchanges:
½ Fat, 1 Meat, 1 Starch,
2 Vegetable

Italian-Style Meat Loaf ⬇CARB

Lean ground beef, lean ground turkey, and egg substitute
make this a much lighter version of a traditional meat loaf.

1 can (6 ounces) no-salt-
   added tomato paste

½ cup water

½ cup dry red wine

1 teaspoon minced garlic

½ teaspoon dried basil

½ teaspoon dried oregano

¼ teaspoon salt

¾ pound 95% lean ground
   beef

¾ pound 93% lean ground
   turkey breast

1 cup fresh whole wheat
   bread crumbs (2 slices
   whole wheat bread)

½ cup shredded zucchini

¼ cup cholesterol-free
   egg substitute or 2 egg
   whites

1. Preheat oven to 350°F. Combine tomato paste, water, wine, garlic, basil, oregano and salt in small saucepan. Bring to a boil; reduce heat to low. Simmer, uncovered, 15 minutes.

2. Combine beef, turkey, bread crumbs, zucchini, egg substitute and ½ cup tomato mixture in large bowl; mix lightly. Shape into loaf; place in ungreased 9×5-inch loaf pan.

3. Bake 45 minutes. Drain fat. Spread remaining tomato mixture over meat loaf. Bake 15 minutes or until cooked through (160°F). Place on serving platter; cool 10 minutes before cutting into 8 slices.

**MAKES
8 SERVINGS**

Calories: 187
Total Fat: 6 g
Saturated Fat: 2 g
Protein: 19 g
Carbohydrate: 12 g
Cholesterol: 56 mg
Fiber: 2 g
Sodium: 212 mg

Dietary Exchanges:
2 Meat, 1 Starch

Yankee Pot Roast and Vegetables

Using reduced-sodium beef broth makes this a low-sodium comfort dish.

1 beef chuck pot roast
(2½ pounds)

Salt and black pepper
(optional)

3 unpeeled baking
potatoes (about
1 pound), cut into
quarters

2 carrots, cut into ¾-inch
slices

2 celery stalks, cut into
¾-inch slices

1 onion, sliced

1 parsnip, cut into ¾-inch
slices

2 bay leaves

1 teaspoon dried
rosemary

½ teaspoon dried thyme

½ cup reduced-sodium
beef broth

MAKES 10 TO 12 SERVINGS

Calories: 270
Total Fat: 10 g
Saturated Fat: 4 g
Protein: 28 g
Carbohydrate: 15 g
Cholesterol: 75 mg
Fiber: 3 g
Sodium: 99 mg

Dietary Exchanges:
1 Fat, 3 Meat, 1 Starch

Slow Cooker Directions

1. Trim and discard excess fat from beef. Cut into ¾-inch pieces; sprinkle with salt and pepper, if desired.

2. Combine potatoes, carrots, celery, onion, parsnip, bay leaves, rosemary and thyme in slow cooker. Top with beef. Pour broth over beef. Cover; cook on LOW 8½ to 9 hours or until beef is fork-tender.

3. Transfer beef and vegetables to serving platter. Remove and discard bay leaves.

Note: To make gravy, ladle the juices into a 2-cup measure; let stand 5 minutes. Skim off fat. Measure remaining juices and heat to a boil in small saucepan. For each cup of juices, mix 2 tablespoons flour with ¼ cup cold water in small bowl until smooth; add to boiling juices. Cook and stir constantly 1 minute or until thickened.

Cheesy Tuna Mac

Reduced-fat cheese slashes calories and fat but adds plenty of creamy flavor.

8 ounces uncooked elbow macaroni

2 tablespoons reduced-fat margarine

2 tablespoons all-purpose flour

¼ teaspoon salt

1 teaspoon paprika

1 cup canned reduced-sodium chicken broth

6 ounces reduced-fat reduced-sodium pasteurized processed cheese product, cut into cubes

1 can (6 ounces) tuna packed in water, drained and flaked

1. Cook macaroni according to package directions, omitting any salt or fat. Drain; set aside.

2. Melt margarine in medium saucepan over medium heat. Add flour, salt and paprika; cook and stir 1 minute. Add broth; bring to a simmer for 2 minutes or until sauce thickens.

3. Add cheese; cook and stir until cheese melts. Combine tuna and pasta in medium bowl; pour sauce mixture over tuna mixture; toss to coat. Sprinkle with additional paprika.

MAKES 4 SERVINGS

Calories: 284
Total Fat: 10 g
Saturated Fat: 3 g
Protein: 27 g
Carbohydrate: 21 g
Cholesterol: 34 mg
Fiber: 1 g
Sodium: 448 mg

Dietary Exchanges:
3 Meat, 1½ Starch

Crispy Baked Chicken

Wheat germ replaces bread crumbs for much less sodium.

8 ounces (1 cup) fat-free French onion dip

½ cup fat-free (skim) milk

1 cup cornflake crumbs

½ cup wheat germ

6 boneless skinless chicken breasts or thighs (about 1½ pounds)

MAKES 6 SERVINGS

Calories: 253
Total Fat: 2 g
Saturated Fat: <1 g
Protein: 35 g
Carbohydrate: 22 g
Cholesterol: 66 mg
Fiber: 1 g
Sodium: 437 mg

Dietary Exchanges:
3 Meat, 1½ Starch

1. Preheat oven to 350°F. Spray shallow baking pan with nonstick cooking spray.

2. Place dip in shallow bowl; stir until smooth. Add milk, 1 tablespoon at a time, until pourable consistency is reached.

3. Combine cornflake crumbs and wheat germ on plate.

4. Dip chicken pieces in milk mixture, then roll in cornflake mixture. Place chicken in single layer in prepared pan. Bake 45 to 50 minutes or until juices run clear when chicken is pierced with fork and chicken is no longer pink in center.

Ethnic Plates

Thai Grilled Chicken

Skinless chicken breasts have less total fat and saturated fat than chicken with skin.

- 4 boneless skinless chicken breasts (about 1¼ pounds)
- ¼ cup reduced-sodium soy sauce
- 2 teaspoons minced garlic
- ½ teaspoon red pepper flakes
- 2 tablespoons honey
- 1 tablespoon fresh lime juice

1. Prepare grill for direct cooking. Place chicken in shallow baking dish. Combine soy sauce, garlic and pepper flakes in small bowl. Pour over chicken, turning to coat. Let stand 10 minutes.

2. Meanwhile, combine honey and lime juice in small bowl; blend well. Set aside.

3. Place chicken on grid over medium coals; brush with marinade. Discard remaining marinade. Grill, covered, 5 minutes. Brush both sides of chicken with honey mixture. Grill 5 minutes more or until chicken is no longer pink in center.

Serving Suggestion: Serve with steamed white rice or Asian vegetables, if your diet permits.

MAKES 4 SERVINGS

Calories: 140, Total Fat: 1 g, Saturated Fat: <1 g, Protein: 22 g, Carbohydrate: 10 g, Cholesterol: 53 mg, Fiber: <1 g, Sodium: 349 mg

Dietary Exchanges: 1 Fruit, 3 Meat

Light Greek Spanakopita

Egg substitute and reduced-fat feta cheese save fat and cholesterol.

1 teaspoon olive oil

1 large onion, cut into quarters and sliced

2 cloves garlic, minced

1 package (10 ounces) frozen chopped spinach, thawed and squeezed dry

½ cup crumbled reduced-fat feta cheese

5 sheets phyllo dough, thawed*

   Olive oil nonstick cooking spray

½ cup cholesterol-free egg substitute

¼ teaspoon nutmeg

¼ to ½ teaspoon black pepper

⅛ teaspoon salt

Thaw entire package of phyllo dough overnight in refrigerator.

MAKES 4 SERVINGS

Calories: 172
Total Fat: 6 g
Saturated Fat: 2 g
Protein: 10 g
Carbohydrate: 18 g
Cholesterol: 5 mg
Fiber: 3 g
Sodium: 580 mg

Dietary Exchanges:
1 Fat, 1 Starch

1. Preheat oven to 375°F. Coat 8-inch square baking pan with cooking spray.

2. Heat oil in large nonstick skillet over medium heat. Add onion; cook and stir 7 to 8 minutes or until soft. Add garlic; cook and stir 30 seconds. Add spinach and cheese; cook and stir until spinach is heated through. Remove from heat.

3. Place 1 sheet phyllo dough on counter with long side toward you. (Cover remaining sheets with damp towel until needed.) Spray right half of phyllo with cooking spray; fold left half over sprayed half. Place sheet in prepared pan. (Two edges will hang over sides of pan.) Spray top of sheet. Spray and fold 2 more sheets of phyllo the same way. Place sheets in pan at 90° angles so edges will hang over all 4 sides of pan. Spray each sheet after it is placed in pan.

4. Combine egg substitute, nutmeg, pepper and salt in small bowl. Stir into spinach mixture until blended. Spread filling over phyllo in pan. Spray and fold 1 sheet phyllo as above; place on top of filling, tucking ends under filling. Bring all overhanging edges of phyllo over top sheet; spray lightly. Spray and fold last sheet as above; place over top sheet, tucking ends under. Spray lightly. Bake 25 to 27 minutes or until top is barely browned. Cool 10 to 15 minutes before serving.

Beef Fajitas

Whole wheat tortillas add more fiber than traditional white flour tortillas.

1 teaspoon ground cumin

1 teaspoon dried oregano

¾ pound well-trimmed boneless beef top sirloin steak (about ¾ inch thick)

2 bell peppers (red, yellow, green or a combination) cut into thin 1-inch strips

½ cup thinly sliced yellow or red onion

4 cloves garlic, minced

Nonstick cooking spray

½ cup jalapeño-flavored salsa

4 (7-inch) high-fiber whole wheat flour tortillas, warmed

¼ cup chopped fresh cilantro

1. Rub cumin and oregano over both sides of steak. Coat large skillet with nonstick cooking spray. Heat over medium heat. Add steak; cook 3 to 4 minutes per side for medium-rare doneness. Transfer steak to carving board; tent with foil and let stand.

2. Add bell peppers, onion and garlic to same skillet. Coat with nonstick cooking spray and cook and stir 4 to 5 minutes or until vegetables are crisp-tender. Add salsa; simmer 3 minutes.

3. Carve steak into thin slices and return to skillet. Toss well and heat through, about 1 minute. Spoon mixture down center of tortillas; top with cilantro and fold in half.

Tip: Tenting with foil is a way to allow grilled meat to continue to cook, without overcooking, while you prepare the rest of a recipe. To tent: drape a large sheet of foil over cooked meat, fold the foil slightly and let it sit loosely over the meat.

MAKES 4 SERVINGS

Calories: 240
Total Fat: 7 g
Saturated Fat: 2 g
Protein: 29 g
Carbohydrate: 28 g
Cholesterol: 35 mg
Fiber: 15 g
Sodium: 610 mg

Dietary Exchanges:
2½ Meat, 1½ Vegetable

Thai Chicken Satays ⬇

Low-fat yogurt is a healthy replacement for a fattening marinade.

1 cup plain low-fat yogurt, plus additional for topping (optional)

½ cup coconut milk

1 tablespoon curry powder

1 teaspoon lemon juice

1 teaspoon grated fresh ginger

½ teaspoon salt

½ teaspoon black pepper

1 clove garlic, crushed

1 pound chicken tenders

6 (6-inch) pita bread rounds, cut in half

Chopped fresh cilantro

1. Combine yogurt, coconut milk, curry, lemon juice, ginger, salt, pepper and garlic in medium bowl; reserve ⅓ cup marinade. Add chicken to remaining marinade; cover and refrigerate at least 8 hours.

2. Soak 12 (10-inch) wooden skewers in water 30 minutes; set aside.

3. Remove chicken from marinade; discard marinade. Thread chicken onto skewers. Place skewers on broiler rack coated with nonstick cooking spray; place rack on broiler pan. Broil 4 to 5 inches from heat source 4 to 5 minutes. Turn skewers; brush with reserved marinade. Discard any remaining marinade. Broil 4 minutes more or until chicken is no longer pink in center.

4. Remove chicken from skewers. Cut pita rounds in half; fill pitas with chicken and top with cilantro and dollop of yogurt, if desired.

**MAKES
6 SERVINGS**
(2 FILLED PITA
HALVES PER
SERVING)

Calories: 271
Total Fat: 3 g
Saturated Fat: 2 g
Protein: 24 g
Carbohydrate: 35 g
Cholesterol: 44 mg
Fiber: 2 g
Sodium: 426 mg

Dietary Exchanges:
2½ Meat, 2 Starch

Turkey and Bean Tostadas

Low-fat toppings like lean turkey, beans, low-fat cheese, and reduced-fat sour cream makes this a healthful, yet satisfying main dish.

6 (8-inch) flour tortillas

1 pound 93% lean ground turkey

1 can (15 ounces) red beans in chili sauce

½ teaspoon chili powder

3 cups washed and shredded romaine lettuce

1 large tomato, chopped

¼ cup chopped fresh cilantro

¼ cup (1 ounce) shredded reduced-fat Monterey Jack cheese

½ cup reduced-fat sour cream (optional)

1. Preheat oven to 350°F. Place tortillas on baking sheets. Bake 7 minutes or until crisp. Place on individual plates.

2. Heat large nonstick skillet over medium-high heat. Add turkey. Cook and stir until turkey is browned; drain. Add beans and chili powder. Cook 5 minutes over medium heat. Divide turkey mixture evenly among tortillas. Top with remaining ingredients and sour cream, if desired.

MAKES 6 SERVINGS

Calories: 288
Total Fat: 10 g
Saturated Fat: 2 g
Protein: 19 g
Carbohydrate: 34 g
Cholesterol: 30 mg
Fiber: 2 g
Sodium: 494 mg

Dietary Exchanges:
2 Meat, 2 Starch, 1 Vegetable

Fiesta Beef Enchiladas

Filling enchiladas with lean beef and low-fat cheese make them healthier than most.

1 pound 95% lean ground beef

½ cup sliced green onions

2 teaspoons minced garlic

1½ cups chopped tomatoes, divided

1 cup cooked white or brown rice

1 cup (4 ounces) shredded reduced-fat Mexican cheese blend or Cheddar cheese, divided

¾ cup frozen corn, thawed

½ cup salsa or picante sauce

12 (6 to 7 inch) corn tortillas

1 can (10 ounces) enchilada sauce

1 cup shredded romaine lettuce

1. Preheat oven to 375°F. Coat 13X9-inch baking dish with nonstick cooking spray.

2. Brown beef 6 to 8 minutes in medium nonstick skillet over medium-high heat, stirring to break up meat. Drain fat. Add green onions and garlic; cook and stir 2 minutes.

3. Add 1 cup tomatoes, rice, ½ cup cheese, corn and salsa to meat mixture; mix well. Spoon mixture down center of tortillas. Roll up; place seam side down in prepared dish. Spoon enchilada sauce evenly over enchiladas.

4. Cover with foil; bake 20 minutes or until heated through. Sprinkle with remaining ½ cup cheese; bake 5 minutes or until cheese melts. Top with lettuce and remaining ⅓ cup tomatoes.

MAKES 6 SERVINGS
(2 ENCHILADAS PER SERVING)

Calories: 341, Total Fat: 11 g, Saturated Fat: 5 g, Protein: 17 g, Carbohydrate: 43 g, Cholesterol: 38 mg, Fiber: 4 g, Sodium: 465 mg

Dietary Exchanges: 1 Fat, 2 Meat, 2 Starch, 2 Vegetable

Fresh Vegetable Lasagna

Low-fat cottage cheese, buttermilk, fat-free yogurt, and egg whites create a creamy filling with barely any fat.

8 ounces uncooked lasagna noodles

1 package (10 ounces) frozen chopped spinach, thawed and squeezed dry

1 cup shredded carrots

½ cup sliced green onions

½ cup sliced red bell pepper (1-inch pieces)

¼ cup chopped fresh parsley

½ teaspoon black pepper

1½ cups low-fat (1%) cottage cheese

½ to 1 cup buttermilk

¼ cup plain fat free yogurt

2 egg whites

1 cup sliced mushrooms

1 can (14 ounces) artichoke hearts, rinsed, drained and chopped

2 cups (8 ounces) shredded part-skim mozzarella cheese

¼ cup grated Parmesan cheese

1. Cook pasta according to package directions, omitting any salt or fat; drain. Rinse under cold water; drain well. Set aside.

2. Preheat oven to 375°F. Combine spinach, carrots, green onions, bell pepper, parsley and black pepper in large bowl; set aside.

3. Combine cottage cheese, buttermilk, yogurt and egg whites in food processor or blender. Cover; process until smooth.

4. Spray 13×9-inch baking pan with nonstick cooking spray. Arrange one third of lasagna noodles in bottom of pan. Spread with half of cottage cheese mixture, half of vegetable mixture, half of mushrooms, half of artichokes and ¾ cup mozzarella. Repeat layers, ending with noodles. Sprinkle with remaining ½ cup mozzarella and Parmesan.

5. Cover; bake 30 minutes. Remove cover; continue baking 20 minutes or until bubbly and heated through. Let stand 10 minutes. Cut into 8 pieces to serve.

MAKES 8 SERVINGS

Calories: 287, Total Fat: 7 g, Saturated Fat: 4 g, Protein: 23 g, Carbohydrate: 33 g, Cholesterol: 22 mg, Fiber: 3 g, Sodium: 568 mg

Dietary Exchanges: ½ Fat, 2 Meat, 1 Starch, 3 Vegetable

Three-Cheese Manicotti

Meatless pasta sauce with fat-free and reduced-fat cheeses make a low-cholesterol dish.

1 cup sliced baby bella mushrooms

2 cups reduced-sodium pasta sauce (without meat)

1 cup fat-free ricotta cheese

¼ cup grated Parmesan cheese

¼ cup cholesterol-free egg substitute

1 tablespoon chopped fresh basil, plus additional for garnish (optional)

⅛ teaspoon salt

¼ teaspoon black pepper

6 cooked manicotti shells

¼ cup shredded reduced-fat mozzarella cheese

1. Preheat oven to 350°F. Coat large skillet with nonstick cooking spray. Add mushrooms and cook over medium heat 5 minutes or until tender. Stir into pasta sauce. Spoon ½ cup pasta sauce (with mushrooms) in bottom of 11×7-inch glass baking dish.

2. Combine ricotta cheese, Parmesan cheese, egg substitute, basil, salt and pepper in medium bowl. Stir well. Spoon about ¼ cup mixture evenly into slightly cooled manicotti shells. Fit shells on top of pasta sauce in baking dish (they should fit snugly). Spoon remaining pasta sauce over manicotti. Cover dish loosely with aluminum foil.

3. Bake 28 to 30 minutes or until sauce is bubbly. Remove from oven and remove foil. Sprinkle with mozzarella cheese. Return to oven 5 to 10 minutes, or until cheese melts. Remove from oven and set aside 2 minutes for manicotti to firm up. Garnish with basil, if desired.

MAKES 6 SERVINGS
(1 MANICOTTI PER SERVING)

Calories: 193
Total Fat: 6 g
Saturated Fat: 2 g
Protein: 11 g
Carbohydrate: 23 g
Cholesterol: 15 mg
Fiber: 3 g
Sodium: 263 mg

Dietary Exchanges:
½ Fat, 1 Meat,
1 Starch, 1 Vegetable

Moroccan-Style Lamb Chops

Lean lamb can be a healthy and low-carbohydrate meal.

1 tablespoon olive oil

1 teaspoon ground cumin

1 teaspoon ground coriander

¾ teaspoon salt

⅛ teaspoon ground cinnamon

⅛ teaspoon ground red pepper

4 center-cut lamb loin chops, cut 1 inch thick (about 1 pound total)

2 cloves garlic, minced

1. Prepare grill or preheat broiler.

2. Combine oil, cumin, coriander, salt, cinnamon and red pepper in small bowl; mix well. Rub or brush oil mixture over both sides of lamb chops. Sprinkle garlic over both sides of lamb chops. Grill on covered grill, or broil 4 to 5 inches from heat, 5 minutes per side for medium doneness.

Hint: This recipe also works well with an indoor electric countertop grill.

MAKES 4 SERVINGS

Calories: 173, Total Fat: 8 g, Saturated Fat: 2 g, Protein: 23 g, Carbohydrate: <1 g, Cholesterol: 71 mg, Fiber: <1 g, Sodium: 510 mg

Dietary Exchanges: 3 Meat

Chicken & Spinach Quesadillas with Pico de Gallo

Fresh vegetables increase the fiber and help keep the fat low.

2 cups chopped seeded tomatoes (2 medium), divided

1 cup chopped green onions, divided

½ cup minced fresh cilantro

1 tablespoon minced jalapeño pepper*

1 tablespoon fresh lime juice

1 cup packed chopped stemmed spinach

1 cup shredded cooked boneless skinless chicken breast

10 (8-inch) fat-free flour tortillas

¾ cup (3 ounces) shredded reduced-fat Cheddar cheese

*Jalapeño peppers can sting and irritate the skin, so wear rubber gloves when handling peppers and do not touch your eyes.

1. Combine 1½ cups tomatoes, ¾ cup green onions, cilantro, jalapeño and lime juice in medium bowl; set aside.

2. Divide remaining ½ cup tomatoes, ¼ cup green onions, spinach and chicken among 5 tortillas; sprinkle with cheese. Top with remaining 5 tortillas.

3. Coat large skillet with nonstick cooking spray. Cook quesadillas, 1 at a time, over medium heat 2 minutes per side or until lightly browned and cheese is melted. Cut each quesadilla into 4 wedges and serve with pico de gallo.

MAKES 5 SERVINGS
(1 QUESADILLA [4 WEDGES] WITH ABOUT ½ CUP PICO DE GALLO PER SERVING)

Calories: 294, Total Fat: 5 g, Saturated Fat: 2 g, Protein: 22 g, Carbohydrate: 54 g, Cholesterol: 34 mg, Fiber: 18 g, Sodium: 540 mg

Dietary Exchanges: 1½ Meat, 2 Starch

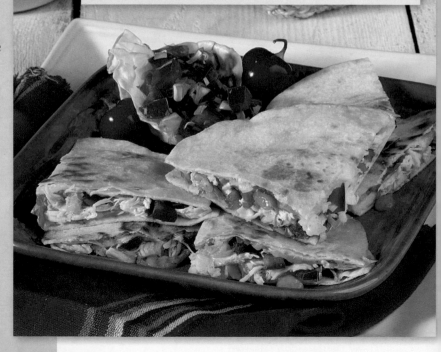

Greek Chicken & Spinach Rice Casserole

Spinach and brown rice add fiber to an authentic entrée.

1 cup finely chopped onion

1 package (10 ounces) frozen chopped spinach, thawed and squeezed dry

1 cup uncooked quick-cooking brown rice

1 cup water

¼ teaspoon salt

⅛ teaspoon ground red pepper

¾ pound chicken tenders

2 teaspoons dried Greek seasoning (oregano, rosemary and sage mixture)

½ teaspoon salt-free lemon-pepper seasoning

1 tablespoon olive oil

1 lemon, cut into wedges

1. Preheat oven to 350°F. Lightly coat large ovenproof skillet with nonstick cooking spray; heat over medium heat. Add onion; cook and stir 2 minutes or until translucent. Add spinach, rice, water, salt and red pepper. Stir until well blended. Remove from heat.

2. Place chicken on top of mixture in skillet in single layer. Sprinkle with Greek seasoning and lemon-pepper seasoning. Cover with foil. Bake 25 minutes or until chicken is no longer pink in center.

3. Remove foil. Drizzle oil evenly over top. Serve with lemon wedges.

MAKES 4 SERVINGS

Calories: 334
Total Fat: 6 g
Saturated Fat: <1 g
Protein: 26 g
Carbohydrate: 45 g
Cholesterol: 49 mg
Fiber: 6 g
Sodium: 535 mg

Dietary Exchanges:
2 Meat, 3 Starch

Eggplant Parmesan

Parmesan cheese is naturally low in fat,
but reduced-fat Parmesan is an even better choice.

2 large egg whites

2 tablespoons water

6 tablespoons Italian-
seasoned bread
crumbs

6 tablespoons reduced-
fat grated Parmesan
cheese, divided

1 large eggplant, peeled
and cut into 12 round
slices

Nonstick cooking spray

2 teaspoons olive oil

1 small onion, diced

1 clove garlic, minced

2 cans (14 ounces each)
no-salt-added diced
tomatoes

½ teaspoon dried basil

½ teaspoon dried oregano

½ cup (2 ounces) shredded
part-skim mozzarella
cheese

1. Preheat oven to 350°F. Coat large rimmed baking pan with nonstick cooking spray.

2. Whisk together egg whites and water in shallow dish. Combine bread crumbs and 2 tablespoons Parmesan cheese in another dish. Dip eggplant slices in egg white mixture, then in bread crumb mixture, pressing lightly to adhere crumbs.

3. Place eggplant slices in single layer in baking pan. Lightly coat tops with cooking spray; bake 25 to 30 minutes, until bottoms are browned. Turn slices; bake 10 to 15 minutes longer or until well browned.

4. To make sauce, heat oil in medium nonstick skillet over medium-high heat. Cook onion until softened, about 5 minutes. Add garlic; cook and stir 1 minute. Stir in tomatoes, basil and oregano; bring to a boil. Reduce heat to a simmer, stir occasionally until sauce is thickened, 15 to 20 minutes.

5. Coat 15×10-inch baking dish with cooking spray. Spread sauce in dish. Arrange eggplant slices in single layer on top of sauce. Combine mozzarella and remaining Parmesan cheese; sprinkle evenly on top. Bake until sauce is bubbly and cheese melts, about 15 to 20 minutes.

Tip: Cut eggplant slices ½ to ¼ inch thick for best results.

MAKES 4 SERVINGS

Calories: 227, Total Fat: 8 g, Saturated Fat: 2 g, Protein: 12 g, Carbohydrate: 31 g, Cholesterol: 11 mg, Fiber: 9 g, Sodium: 610 mg

Dietary Exchanges: ½ Fat, 2 Meat, 2 Starch

Thai-Style Beef with Pasta on Lettuce

Fresh vegetables and lean beef enhance flavor and cut fat and calories.

3 tablespoons orange juice

2 tablespoons creamy peanut butter

2 tablespoons reduced-sodium soy sauce

1 tablespoon rice wine vinegar

2 teaspoons grated fresh ginger

6 ounces uncooked whole wheat spaghetti, broken in half

½ pound 96% lean ground beef

2 teaspoons minced garlic

2 cups (about 4 ounces) thinly sliced bok choy

½ cup (about 2 ounces) coarsely chopped carrot

4 green onions, cut into 1-inch pieces

¼ teaspoon crushed red pepper

6 pieces leaf lettuce

2 tablespoons (½ ounce) lightly salted dry roasted peanuts

1. Process orange juice, peanut butter, soy sauce, vinegar and ginger in food processor or blender until nearly smooth. Set aside.

2. Cook spaghetti according to package directions, omitting any salt or fat. Drain and set aside.

3. Meanwhile, cook beef and garlic 6 to 8 minutes in large nonstick skillet over medium-high heat until meat is brown, stirring to break up meat. Drain fat. Stir in bok choy, carrot, green onions and red pepper. Drizzle with orange juice mixture. Reduce heat to medium; cover and cook 2 minutes.

4. Add hot spaghetti; toss until combined. Place lettuce leaves on serving plates. Spoon noodle mixture onto leaves and sprinkle with peanuts.

MAKES 6 SERVINGS

Calories: 219, Total Fat: 7 g, Saturated Fat: 2 g, Protein: 15 g, Carbohydrate: 27 g, Cholesterol: 23 mg, Fiber: 1 g, Sodium: 285 mg

Dietary Exchanges: ½ Fat, 1 Meat, 2 Starch

Mexican Casserole with Tortilla Chips

*Baked (instead of fried) tortilla chips are
the perfect low-fat topping to this flavorful dish.*

12 ounces lean ground
   turkey

1 can (about 14 ounces)
   no-salt-added stewed
   tomatoes

1 bag (8 ounces) frozen
   bell pepper stir-fry
   mixture, thawed

¾ teaspoon ground cumin

½ teaspoon salt (optional)

1½ ounces finely shredded
   reduced-fat sharp
   Cheddar cheese

2 ounces reduced-
   fat tortilla
   chips, lightly
   crushed

MAKES
4 SERVINGS

Calories: 244
Total Fat: 9 g
Saturated Fat: 3 g
Protein: 23 g
Carbohydrate: 21 g
Cholesterol: 60 mg
Fiber: 3 g
Sodium: 236 mg

Dietary Exchanges:
1 Fat, 1 Meat, 2 Starch,
1 Vegetable

1. Coat large skillet with nonstick cooking spray. Cook turkey over medium heat until no longer pink, stirring to break up meat. Stir in tomatoes, pepper mixture and cumin; bring to a boil. Reduce heat; cover and simmer 20 minutes or until vegetables are tender.

2. Remove from heat and stir in salt, if desired. Sprinkle evenly with cheese and chips.

Variation: Sprinkle chips into a casserole. Spread cooked turkey mixture evenly over the chips and top with cheese.

Shrimp and Chicken Paella

Shrimp and chicken are lean protein sources and make this a very low-fat recipe.

¾ cup ready-to-serve rice

2 cans (about 14 ounces each) no-salt-added diced tomatoes, undrained, divided

½ teaspoon ground turmeric or ⅛ teaspoon saffron threads

1 package (¾ pound) frozen peeled, deveined shrimp, thawed (about 3 cups)

2 chicken tenders (about 4 ounces), cut into 1-inch pieces

1 cup frozen peas

1. Preheat oven to 400°F. Lightly coat 8-inch square glass baking dish with nonstick cooking spray. Spread rice in prepared dish.

2. Pour 1 can tomatoes with their juices over rice; sprinkle turmeric over tomatoes. Arrange shrimp and chicken over tomatoes. Top with peas.

3. Drain remaining can of tomatoes, discarding juice. Arrange tomatoes evenly over shrimp and chicken. Cover; bake 30 minutes. Let stand, covered, 5 minutes before serving. To serve, spoon into shallow, rimmed bowls.

**MAKES
4 SERVINGS**
(1 CUP PER SERVING)

Calories: 175
Total Fat: 1 g
Saturated Fat: <1 g
Protein: 19 g
Carbohydrate: 19 g
Cholesterol: 97 mg
Fiber: 2 g
Sodium: 152 mg

Dietary Exchanges:
2 Meat, 1 Starch, 1 Vegetable

Fettuccine Alfredo

This simple plate is made healthy by replacing cream with skim milk.

- 2 teaspoons reduced-fat margarine
- 3 cloves garlic, finely chopped
- 4½ teaspoons all-purpose flour
- 1½ cups fat-free (skim) milk
- ½ cup grated Parmesan cheese
- 3½ teaspoons Neufchâtel cheese
- ¼ teaspoon white pepper
- 4 ounces fettuccine, cooked without salt, drained and kept hot
- ¼ cup chopped fresh parsley

Melt margarine in medium saucepan. Add garlic. Cook and stir 1 minute. Stir in flour. Gradually stir in milk. Cook until sauce thickens, stirring constantly. Add cheeses and pepper; cook until melted. Serve on fettuccine; top with parsley.

MAKES 4 SERVINGS

Calories: 242, Total Fat: 9 g, Saturated Fat: 4 g, Protein: 14 g, Carbohydrate: 27 g, Cholesterol: 18 mg, Fiber: 1 g, Sodium: 344 mg

Dietary Exchanges: ½ Fat, ½ Meat, ½ Milk, 2 Starch

Thai Pasta Salad with Peanut Sauce

The extra fiber and protein in whole wheat spaghetti make it more filling for less calories than regular spaghetti.

¼ cup evaporated skimmed milk

1 tablespoon plus 1½ teaspoons creamy peanut butter

1 tablespoon plus 1½ teaspoons finely chopped red onion

1 teaspoon lemon juice

¾ teaspoon brown sugar

½ teaspoon reduced-sodium soy sauce

⅛ teaspoon red pepper flakes

½ teaspoon finely chopped fresh ginger

1 cup hot cooked whole wheat spaghetti

2 teaspoons finely chopped green onion

MAKES 2 SERVINGS

Calories: 187
Total Fat: 6 g
Saturated Fat: 1 g
Protein: 9 g
Carbohydrate: 27 g
Cholesterol: 38 mg
Fiber: 3 g
Sodium: 85 mg

Dietary Exchanges:
1 Fat, ½ Milk, 1½ Starch

1. Combine milk, peanut butter, red onion, lemon juice, brown sugar, soy sauce and red pepper flakes in medium saucepan. Bring to a boil over high heat, stirring constantly. Boil 2 minutes, stirring constantly. Reduce heat to medium-low. Add ginger; blend well.

2. Remove from heat and add spaghetti to sauce; toss to coat. Top servings with green onion.

Tip: When buying fresh ginger, select roots with smooth, unwrinkled skin. To use, peel the tough skin away to expose the tender root underneath; peel only as needed.

Mediterranean Chicken Kabobs

A low-fat and low-sodium marinade create a nutritious main dish.

2 pounds boneless skinless chicken breasts or chicken tenders, cut into 1-inch pieces

1 small eggplant, peeled and cut into 1-inch pieces

1 medium zucchini, cut crosswise into ½-inch slices

2 medium onions, each cut into 8 wedges

16 medium mushrooms, stems removed

16 cherry tomatoes

1 cup fat-free reduced-sodium chicken broth

⅔ cup balsamic vinegar

3 tablespoons olive oil

2 tablespoons dried mint

4 teaspoons dried basil

1 tablespoon dried oregano

2 teaspoons grated lemon peel

Chopped fresh parsley (optional)

4 cups hot cooked couscous

1. Alternately thread chicken, eggplant, zucchini, onions, mushrooms and tomatoes onto 16 metal skewers; place in large glass baking dish.

2. Combine chicken broth, vinegar, oil, mint, basil and oregano in small bowl; pour over kabobs. Cover; marinate in refrigerator 2 hours, turning occasionally. Remove kabobs from marinade; discard marinade.

3. Preheat broiler. Broil kabobs 6 inches from heat 10 to 15 minutes or until chicken is cooked through, turning kabobs halfway through cooking time.

4. Stir lemon peel and parsley, if desired, into couscous; serve with kabobs.

Tip: These kabobs can be grilled instead of broiled. Spray the grill grid with nonstick cooking spray, then prepare the grill for direct cooking. Grill the kabobs, covered, over medium-hot coals 10 to 15 minutes or until the chicken is cooked through. Turn the kabobs halfway through the cooking time.

MAKES 8 SERVINGS
(2 KABOBS WITH ½ CUP COOKED COUSCOUS PER SERVING)

Calories: 300, Total Fat: 5 g, Saturated Fat: 1 g, Protein: 31 g, Carbohydrate: 32 g, Cholesterol: 69 mg, Fiber: 4 g, Sodium: 79 mg

Dietary Exchanges: 3 Meat, 1 Starch, 3 Vegetable

Appetizers, Sides, and Snacks

Bacon & Onion Cheese Ball

Fat-free cream cheese and fat-free sour cream lighten up this savory dip.

1 package (8 ounces) fat-free cream cheese, softened

½ cup fat-free sour cream

½ cup real bacon bits

½ cup chopped green onions

¼ cup (1 ounce) blue cheese crumbles

Additional sliced green onion (optional)

Celery sticks or whole wheat crackers (optional)

1. Combine cream cheese, sour cream, bacon bits, green onions and blue cheese in large bowl until well blended.

2. Shape mixture into a ball. Wrap in plastic wrap and chill at least 1 hour before serving. Garnish with additional green onion and serve with celery or crackers, if desired.

MAKES 20 SERVINGS
(2 TABLESPOONS PER SERVING)

Calories: 34, Total Fat: 1 g, Saturated Fat: <1 g, Protein: 4 g, Carbohydrate: 2 g, Cholesterol: 7 mg, Fiber: <1 g, Sodium: 203 mg

Dietary Exchanges: ½ Meat

Spinach-Stuffed Appetizer Shells

This meatless dish is guilt-free thanks to fat-free cheese and reduced-fat mayonnaise.

18 jumbo pasta shells (about 6 ounces)

1 package (10 ounces) frozen chopped spinach, thawed and well drained

1 can (8 ounces) water chestnuts, drained and chopped

¾ cup fat-free ricotta cheese

½ cup reduced-fat mayonnaise

¼ cup finely chopped carrot

3 tablespoons finely chopped onion

¾ teaspoon garlic powder

¾ teaspoon hot pepper sauce

Fresh dill (optional)

1. Cook shells according to package directions, omitting any salt or fat. Rinse under cold running water until shells are cool; drain well.

2. Combine remaining ingredients in medium bowl; mix well.

3. Fill each shell with about 3 tablespoons spinach mixture; cover. Refrigerate up to 12 hours before serving. Garnish with dill, if desired.

MAKES 9 SERVINGS
(2 STUFFED SHELLS PER SERVING)

Calories: 155
Total Fat: 5 g
Saturated Fat: 1 g
Protein: 6 g
Carbohydrate: 21 g
Cholesterol: 2 mg
Fiber: 3 g
Sodium: 172 mg

Dietary Exchanges:
1 Fat, 1 Starch, 1 Vegetable

Favorite Green Beans

Parmesan cheese is lower in fat than most cheeses, and its strong flavor perks up plain green beans.

1 pound green beans
(ends trimmed)

2 tablespoons reduced-fat
margarine

¼ cup grated Parmesan
cheese

1 teaspoon garlic salt

1. Bring 1 quart of water to a boil in large saucepan. Add green beans and boil 3 minutes. Remove from heat and drain.

2. Heat margarine in large skillet over medium heat. Add green beans to skillet and top with cheese and garlic salt. Cook 5 minutes, stirring occasionally. Remove from heat and serve warm.

MAKES 6 SERVINGS (⅔ CUP PER SERVING)

Calories: 75, Total Fat: 5 g, Saturated Fat: 3 g, Protein: 3 g, Carbohydrate: 6 g, Cholesterol: 3 mg, Dietary Fiber: 2 g, Sodium: 96 mg

Dietary Exchanges: 1 Fat, 1 Vegetable

Turkey Meatballs in Cranberry-Barbecue Sauce

Lean ground turkey (instead of beef or pork) makes this a low-fat party favorite.

1 can (16 ounces) jellied cranberry sauce

½ cup barbecue sauce

1 egg white

1 pound 93% lean ground turkey

1 green onion, sliced

2 teaspoons grated orange peel

1 teaspoon reduced-sodium soy sauce

¼ teaspoon black pepper

⅛ teaspoon ground red pepper (optional)

Italian parsley (optional)

Slow Cooker Directions

1. Combine cranberry sauce and barbecue sauce in slow cooker. Cover; cook on HIGH 20 to 30 minutes or until cranberry sauce is melted and mixture is hot.

2. Meanwhile, beat egg white in medium bowl. Add turkey, green onion, orange peel, soy sauce, black pepper and ground red pepper, if desired; mix until well blended. Shape into 24 balls.

3. Coat large skillet with nonstick cooking spray; heat over medium heat. Add meatballs; cook 8 to 10 minutes or until browned on all sides. Add to slow cooker; stir gently to coat with sauce mixture.

4. Turn slow cooker to LOW. Cover; cook 3 hours. Garnish with parsley, if desired, and serve warm.

MAKES 12 SERVINGS
(2 MEATBALLS WITH 2 TABLESPOONS SAUCE PER SERVING)

Calories: 137, Total Fat: 4 g, Saturated Fat: 1 g, Protein: 7 g, Carbohydrate: 18 g, Cholesterol: 19 mg, Fiber: 1 g, Sodium: 206 mg

Dietary Exchanges: ½ Fat, 1 Fruit, 1 Meat

Stuffed Party Baguette

Replacing oily sandwich spreads with fat-free salad dressing is a simple and healthy substitution.

2 medium red bell peppers

1 loaf French bread (about 14 inches long)

¼ cup plus 2 tablespoons fat-free Italian dressing, divided

1 small red onion, very thinly sliced

8 large fresh basil leaves

3 ounces Swiss cheese, very thinly sliced

MAKES 12 SERVINGS
(1 BAGUETTE SLICE PER SERVING)

Calories: 90
Total Fat: 3 g
Saturated Fat: 1 g
Protein: 4 g
Carbohydrate: 14 g
Cholesterol: 7 mg
Fiber: 1 g
Sodium: 239 mg

Dietary Exchanges:
½ Fat, 1 Starch

1. Preheat oven to 425°F. Cover large baking sheet with foil.

2. To roast bell peppers, cut in half; remove stems, seeds and membranes. Place peppers, cut sides down, on prepared baking sheet. Bake 20 to 25 minutes or until skins are browned.

3. Transfer peppers to paper bag; close bag. Let stand 10 minutes or until peppers are cool enough to handle and skins are loosened. Peel off and discard skins; cut peppers into strips.

4. Trim ends from bread. Cut loaf in half lengthwise. Remove soft insides of loaf and reserve for another use.

5. Brush ¼ cup Italian dressing evenly onto cut sides of bread. Arrange pepper strips on bottom half of loaf; top with onion. Brush onion with remaining 2 tablespoons Italian dressing; top with basil and cheese. Replace bread top. Wrap loaf tightly in plastic wrap; refrigerate at least 2 hours.

6. To serve, remove plastic wrap. Cut loaf crosswise into 1-inch slices. Secure with toothpicks.

Steamed Pork Wontons with Sweet Soy Dipping Sauce

Wonton wrappers are surprisingly low in fat and make perfect low-carbohydrate appetizers.

WONTONS

8 ounces lean ground pork

¼ cup chopped fresh cilantro

1½ tablespoons grated fresh ginger

1 teaspoon grated orange peel

¼ teaspoon ground red pepper

⅛ teaspoon salt

24 wonton wrappers

3 teaspoons vegetable oil, divided

1 cup water, divided

DIPPING SAUCE

2 to 3 tablespoons pourable sugar substitute*

2 tablespoons white vinegar

2 tablespoons lime juice

2 tablespoons reduced-sodium soy sauce

This recipe was tested using sucralose-based sugar substitute.

1. Combine pork, cilantro, ginger, orange peel, red pepper and salt in medium bowl. Place rounded teaspoon in center of each wonton wrapper. Prepare 1 at a time according to package directions, using small amount of water to seal edges.

2. Heat 1½ teaspoons oil in large nonstick skillet over medium-high heat. Add 12 wontons and cook 1 minute or until golden brown on bottom. Add ½ cup water, cover; cook 5 minutes or until water has evaporated. Place on serving platter and cover with foil to keep warm. Repeat with remaining oil, wontons and water.

3. Combine sauce ingredients in small bowl. If desired, microwave sauce on HIGH about 20 to 30 seconds. Serve as dipping sauce.

MAKES 8 SERVINGS
(3 WONTONS AND 1 TABLESPOON SAUCE PER SERVING)

Calories: 135, Total Fat: 6 g, Saturated Fat: 2 g, Protein: 7 g, Carbohydrate: 12 g, Cholesterol: 20 mg, Fiber: <1 g, Sodium: 236 mg

Dietary Exchanges: 1 Meat, 1 Starch

Veggie Quesadilla Appetizers

Chopped vegetables add crunch and bulk to keep calories, carbohydrates, and fat low.

ZESTY PICO DE GALLO

2 cups chopped seeded tomatoes

1 cup chopped green onions

1 can (about 8 ounces) tomato sauce

½ cup minced fresh cilantro

1 to 2 tablespoons minced jalapeño peppers*

1 tablespoon fresh lime juice

QUESADILLAS

10 (8-inch) flour tortillas

1 cup finely chopped broccoli

1 cup thinly sliced small mushrooms

¾ cup shredded carrots

¼ cup chopped green onions

1¼ cups (5 ounces) reduced-fat sharp Cheddar cheese

Jalapeño peppers can sting and irritate the skin, so wear rubber gloves when handling peppers and do not touch your eyes.

1. Combine Zesty Pico de Gallo ingredients in medium bowl. Refrigerate at least 1 hour.

2. Brush both sides of tortillas lightly with water. Heat small nonstick skillet over medium heat. Heat tortillas, 1 at a time, 30 seconds on each side. Divide vegetables among 5 tortillas; sprinkle evenly with cheese. Top with remaining 5 tortillas.

3. Cook quesadillas, 1 at a time, in large nonstick skillet or on griddle over medium heat 2 minutes on each side, or until surface is crisp and cheese is melted. Cut each quesadilla into 4 wedges. Serve with Zesty Pico de Gallo.

MAKES 20 SERVINGS
(1 QUESADILLA WEDGE WITH ABOUT 1½ TABLESPOONS PICO DE GALLO PER SERVING)

Calories: 79, **Total Fat:** 2 g, **Saturated Fat:** 1 g, **Protein:** 4 g, **Carbohydrate:** 12 g, **Cholesterol:** 4 mg, **Fiber:** 1 g, **Sodium:** 223 mg

Dietary Exchanges: 1 Starch

Southern Crab Cakes with Rémoulade Dipping Sauce

Low-fat crab is joined with a healthier version of a classic New Orleans sauce.

10 ounces fresh lump crabmeat

1½ cups fresh white or sourdough bread crumbs, divided

¼ cup chopped green onions

½ cup fat-free or reduced-fat mayonnaise, divided

1 egg white, lightly beaten

2 tablespoons coarse-grained or spicy brown mustard, divided

¾ teaspoon hot pepper sauce, divided

2 teaspoons olive oil, divided

Lemon wedges (optional)

1. Preheat oven to 200°F. Pick out and discard any shell or cartilage from crabmeat. Combine crabmeat, ¾ cup bread crumbs and green onions in medium bowl. Add ¼ cup mayonnaise, egg white, 1 tablespoon mustard and ½ teaspoon hot pepper sauce; mix well. Using ¼ cup mixture per cake, shape into 8 (½-inch-thick) cakes. Roll crab cakes lightly in remaining ¾ cup bread crumbs.

2. Heat large nonstick skillet over medium heat; add 1 teaspoon oil. Add 4 crab cakes; cook 4 to 5 minutes per side or until golden brown. Transfer to serving platter; keep warm in oven. Repeat with remaining 1 teaspoon oil and crab cakes.

3. For dipping sauce, combine remaining ¼ cup mayonnaise, 1 tablespoon mustard and ¼ teaspoon hot pepper sauce in small bowl; mix well.

4. Serve crab cakes warm with dipping sauce and lemon wedges, if desired.

MAKES
8 SERVINGS
(1 CRAB CAKE WITH
1½ TEASPOONS
SAUCE PER SERVING)

Calories: 81
Total Fat: 2 g
Saturated Fat: <1 g
Protein: 7 g
Carbohydrate: 8 g
Cholesterol: 30 mg
Fiber: <1 g
Sodium: 376 mg

Dietary Exchanges:
1 Meat, ½ Starch

Bruschetta

Instead of drowning the bread in oil, only 1 teaspoon is needed to make this low-fat hors d'oeurve.

1 cup thinly sliced onion

½ cup chopped seeded tomato

2 tablespoons capers, drained

¼ teaspoon black pepper

3 cloves garlic, finely chopped

1 teaspoon olive oil

4 slices French bread

½ cup (2 ounces) shredded reduced-fat Monterey Jack cheese

1. Coat large skillet with nonstick cooking spray. Cook and stir onion over medium heat 5 minutes. Stir in tomato, capers and pepper. Cook 3 minutes.

2. Preheat broiler. Combine garlic and olive oil in small bowl. Brush bread slices with oil mixture. Top with onion mixture; sprinkle with cheese. Place on baking sheet. Broil 3 minutes or until cheese melts.

MAKES 4 SERVINGS
(1 SLICE PER SERVING)

Calories: 90, Total Fat: 2 g, Saturated Fat: <1 g, Protein: 3 g, Carbohydrate: 17 g, Cholesterol: 0 mg, Fiber: <1 g, Sodium: 194 mg

Dietary Exchanges: ½ Meat, 1 Starch

Hot Potato Salad

Reduced-fat turkey bacon and light mayonnaise add significant flavor without adding too much fat.

4 slices reduced-fat turkey bacon

1 cup diced yellow onion (about 1 medium)

2 pounds medium potatoes, peeled and cubed

3 tablespoons flour

⅓ teaspoon salt (optional)

¼ cup red wine vinegar

⅓ cup sugar

3 tablespoons light mayonnaise

½ cup diced green onions (optional)

1. Heat large nonstick skillet over medium-high heat. Cook turkey bacon then set aside on separate plate. Add yellow onion to skillet and cook until beginning to brown, stirring frequently. Remove from heat, crumble bacon and return to skillet with yellow onion.

2. Meanwhile, bring 4 cups of water to a boil in large saucepan over high heat. Add potatoes; return to a boil. Reduce heat, cover and simmer 5 to 6 minutes or until tender. Drain and add potatoes to skillet with yellow onion mixture.

3. Whisk together flour, salt, if desired, vinegar, sugar and mayonnaise in small bowl. Pour over potato mixture and mix well to combine. Serve warm and top with diced green onions, if desired.

**MAKES
6 SERVINGS**
(¾ CUP PER SERVING)

Calories: 260
Total Fat: 4 g
Saturated Fat: 1 g
Protein: 5 g
Carbohydrate: 50 g
Cholesterol: 13 mg
Dietary Fiber: 3 g
Sodium: 189 mg

Dietary Exchanges:
1 Fat, 3 Starch

Buffalo Chicken Tenders

A healthy twist on a favorite dish–chicken tenders are baked rather than fried.

3 tablespoons Louisiana-style hot sauce

½ teaspoon paprika

¼ teaspoon ground red pepper

1 pound chicken tenders

½ cup fat-free blue cheese dressing

¼ cup reduced-fat sour cream

2 tablespoons crumbled blue cheese

1 medium green or red bell pepper, cut lengthwise into ½-inch-thick slices

1. Preheat oven to 375°F. Combine hot sauce, paprika and ground red pepper in small bowl; brush over chicken. Place chicken in greased 11X7-inch baking dish. Cover; marinate in refrigerator 30 minutes.

2. Remove from refrigerator and bake, uncovered, about 15 minutes or until chicken is no longer pink in center.

3. Combine blue cheese dressing, sour cream and crumbled blue cheese in small serving bowl. Serve dip with chicken and pepper slices.

**MAKES
10 SERVINGS**

(2 CHICKEN TENDERS PLUS 1½ TABLESPOONS DIPPING SAUCE PER SERVING)

Calories: 83
Total Fat: 2 g
Saturated Fat: 1 g
Protein: 9 g
Carbohydrate: 5 g
Cholesterol: 27 mg
Fiber: 0 g
Sodium: 180 mg

Dietary Exchanges:
1 Meat, ½ Starch

Vegetables and Sun-Dried Tomatoes

Instead of adding a fattening sauce, these vegetables are kept healthy with minimal oil and a sprinkle of salt.

1 pound green beans (ends trimmed)

1 tablespoon olive oil, divided

5 ounces mushrooms, sliced

½ cup toasted sliced almonds

½ cup sun-dried tomatoes, sliced

¼ teaspoon salt

1. Bring large pot of water to a boil. Add green beans and boil 3 minutes. Remove from heat and drain.

2. Heat 2 teaspoons oil in large skillet over medium heat. Add green beans, mushrooms and almonds. Cook and stir 3 minutes. Add sun-dried tomatoes and remaining oil and cook and stir another 2 to 3 minutes. Remove from heat, cover and let stand 15 minutes to absorb flavors. Season with salt before serving.

MAKES 6 SERVINGS
(⅔ CUP PER SERVING)

Calories: 101
Total Fat: 6 g
Saturated Fat: 1 g
Protein: 4 g
Carbohydrate: 11 g
Cholesterol: 0 mg
Dietary Fiber: 4 g
Sodium: 193 mg

Dietary Exchanges:
1 Fat, 2 Vegetable

Angelic Deviled Eggs

Most of the fat-laden egg yolks are replaced with a guiltless filling of low-fat cottage cheese and Dijon mustard.

6 eggs

¼ cup low-fat (1%) cottage cheese

3 tablespoons prepared fat-free ranch dressing

2 teaspoons Dijon mustard

2 tablespoons minced fresh chives or dill

1 tablespoon diced well-drained pimientos or roasted red pepper

MAKES 12 SERVINGS
(1 FILLED EGG HALF PER SERVING)

Calories: 44
Total Fat: 3 g
Saturated Fat: <1 g
Protein: 4 g
Carbohydrate: 1 g
Cholesterol: 27 mg
Fiber: 1 g
Sodium: 96 mg

Dietary Exchanges:
½ Meat

1. Place eggs in medium saucepan; add enough water to cover. Bring to a boil over medium heat. Remove from heat; cover. Let stand 15 minutes. Drain. Add cold water to eggs in saucepan; let stand until eggs are cool. Drain and peel.

2. Slice eggs lengthwise in half. Remove yolks, reserving 3 yolk halves. Discard remaining yolks or reserve for another use. Place egg whites, cut sides up, on serving plate; cover with plastic wrap. Refrigerate while preparing filling.

3. Combine cottage cheese, dressing, mustard and reserved yolk halves in food processor; process until smooth. (Or, place in small bowl and mash with fork until well blended.) Transfer cheese mixture to small bowl; stir in chives and pimientos. Spoon into egg whites. Cover and chill at least 1 hour.

Easy Nachos

Making low-fat nachos is easy by leaving out sour cream and using lean turkey instead of beef.

4 (6-inch) flour tortillas

Nonstick cooking spray

¼ pound 93% lean ground turkey

⅔ cup salsa

2 tablespoons sliced green onion

½ cup (2 ounces) shredded reduced-fat Cheddar cheese

**MAKES
4 SERVINGS**
(8 NACHOS PER SERVING)

Calories: 190
Total Fat: 7 g
Saturated Fat: 3 g
Protein: 13 g
Carbohydrate: 20 g
Cholesterol: 25 mg
Fiber: 2 g
Sodium: 580 mg

Dietary Exchanges:
1 Fat, 1 Meat, 1 Starch, 1 Vegetable

1. Preheat oven to 350°F. Cut each tortilla into 8 wedges; lightly spray one side of wedges with nonstick cooking spray. Place on ungreased baking sheet. Bake 5 to 9 minutes or until lightly browned and crisp.

2. Meanwhile, brown turkey in small nonstick skillet over medium-high heat, stirring to break up meat; drain fat. Stir in salsa; cook until heated through.

3. Spoon turkey mixture evenly over tortilla wedges. Sprinkle with green onion. Top with cheese. Bake 1 to 2 minutes or until cheese melts.

Serving Suggestion: To make these nachos even more special, cut tortillas into shapes with cookie cutters and bake as directed.

Lunch or Dinner Dishes

Autumn Pasta

Bulking up pasta with chicken and fresh vegetables adds protein and fiber without adding too many carbohydrates.

1 boneless skinless chicken breast (about ¼ pound), cut into ½-inch cubes

8 brussels sprouts, trimmed and sliced

1 large bulb fennel, trimmed, quartered and sliced

2 medium tomatoes, seeded and chopped

¼ cup lemon juice

1 tablespoon olive oil

1 teaspoon minced garlic

1 cup cooked whole-grain rotini pasta

2 tablespoons grated Parmesan cheese

1. Combine chicken, brussels sprouts, fennel, tomatoes, lemon juice, oil and garlic in large bowl.

2. Lightly coat large skillet with nonstick cooking spray; heat over medium heat. Add chicken mixture; cook, covered, about 15 minutes or until vegetables are tender and chicken is cooked through.

3. Add pasta to skillet; cook until heated through. Sprinkle each serving with cheese.

MAKES 2 SERVINGS
(2¼ CUPS PER SERVING)

Calories: 315, Total Fat: 10 g, Saturated Fat: 2 g, Protein: 23 g, Carbohydrate: 38 g, Cholesterol: 37 mg, Fiber: 9 g, Sodium: 168 mg

Dietary Exchanges: 2½ Meat, 2 Starch, 1 Vegetable

Chicken Wraps ▼CARB

Using lettuce instead of a tortilla or pancake saves a great deal of carbohydrates.

½ **pound boneless skinless chicken thighs**

½ **teaspoon Chinese five-spice powder***

½ **cup bean sprouts**

2 **tablespoons minced green onion**

2 **tablespoons sliced almonds**

2 **tablespoons reduced-sodium soy sauce**

4 **teaspoons hoisin sauce**

1 to 2 **teaspoons chili garlic sauce****

4 **large lettuce leaves**

*Chinese five-spice powder is usually a blend of cinnamon, cloves, star anise, fennel seed, and Szechuan pepper.

**Chili garlic sauce is available in the Asian foods section of most large supermarkets.

1. Preheat oven to 350°F. Coat baking sheet with nonstick cooking spray.

2. Place chicken on prepared baking sheet; sprinkle with five-spice powder. Bake 20 minutes or until chicken is cooked through. Set aside until cool enough to handle.

3. Dice chicken. Combine chicken, bean sprouts, green onion, almonds, soy sauce, hoisin sauce and chili garlic sauce in large bowl. Spoon ⅓ cup chicken mixture onto each lettuce leaf; roll up.

MAKES 4 SERVINGS

Calories: 114, Total Fat: 5 g, Saturated Fat: 1 g, Protein: 13 g, Carbohydrate: 5 g, Cholesterol: 47 mg, Fiber: 1 g, Sodium: 302 mg

Dietary Exchanges: 1½ Meat, 1 Vegetable

Pasta with Tuna, Green Beans & Tomatoes

Tuna packed in water is high in protein, low in fat, and carbohydrate-free.

8 ounces uncooked whole wheat penne, rigatoni or fusilli pasta

1½ cups frozen cut green beans

3 teaspoons olive oil, divided

3 green onions, sliced

1 clove garlic, minced

1 can (about 14 ounces) diced Italian-style tomatoes, drained or 2 large tomatoes, chopped (about 2 cups)

½ teaspoon salt

½ teaspoon Italian seasoning

¼ teaspoon black pepper

1 can (12 ounces) solid albacore tuna packed in water, drained and flaked

Chopped fresh parsley (optional)

1. Cook pasta according to package directions, omitting any salt or fat. Add green beans during last 7 minutes of cooking time (allow water to return to a boil before resuming timing). Drain and keep warm.

2. Meanwhile, heat 1 teaspoon oil in large skillet over medium heat. Cook and stir green onions and garlic 2 minutes. Add tomatoes, salt, Italian seasoning and pepper; cook and stir 4 to 5 minutes. Add pasta mixture, tuna and remaining oil; mix gently. Garnish with parsley, if desired, and serve immediately.

MAKES 6 SERVINGS
(1¼ CUPS PER SERVING)

Calories: 228, Total Fat: 4 g, Saturated Fat: <1 g, Protein: 15 g, Carbohydrate: 34 g, Cholesterol: 14 mg, Fiber: 3 g, Sodium: 345 mg

Dietary Exchanges: 3 Meat, 2 Starch, 1 Vegetable

Tuna Melts

Reduced-fat mayonnaise and reduced-fat cheese make this dish much lower in fat than a traditional tuna melt.

1 can (12 ounces) reduced-sodium chunk white tuna packed in water, drained and flaked

1½ cups packaged coleslaw mix

3 tablespoons sliced green onions

3 tablespoons reduced-fat mayonnaise

1 tablespoon Dijon mustard

1 teaspoon dried dill weed (optional)

4 English muffins, split and lightly toasted

⅓ cup shredded reduced-fat Cheddar cheese

1. Preheat broiler. Combine tuna, coleslaw mix and green onions in medium bowl. Combine mayonnaise, mustard and dill weed, if desired, in small bowl. Stir mayonnaise mixture into tuna mixture. Spread tuna mixture onto muffin halves. Place on broiler pan.

2. Broil 4 inches from heat 3 to 4 minutes or until heated through. Sprinkle with cheese. Broil 1 to 2 minutes more or until cheese is melted.

MAKES 4 SERVINGS
(2 TOPPED MUFFIN HALVES PER SERVING)

Calories: 294
Total Fat: 6 g
Saturated Fat: 1 g
Protein: 29 g
Carbohydrate: 29 g
Cholesterol: 31 mg
Fiber: 2 g
Sodium: 459 mg

Dietary Exchanges:
3 Meat, 2 Starch

Chicken Salad Pitas

Whole wheat pitas and spring greens make a fresh and high-fiber pita sandwich.

4 cups torn mixed spring greens

2 cups (about ½ pound) chopped cooked chicken breast

½ cup chopped green bell pepper or poblano chile pepper

½ cup reduced-fat ranch dressing

4 whole wheat pita bread rounds, halved

Black pepper (optional)

1. Toss greens, chicken, bell pepper and salad dressing in large bowl. Microwave pita halves on HIGH 12 to 15 seconds.

2. Fill each warmed pita half with equal amount of salad mixture. Sprinkle with black pepper, if desired.

MAKES 4 SERVINGS
(2 PITA HALVES WITH ABOUT 1½ CUPS SALAD MIXTURE PER SERVING)

Calories: 325, Total Fat: 4 g, Saturated Fat: <1 g, Protein: 29 g, Carbohydrate: 44 g, Cholesterol: 54 mg, Fiber: 6 g, Sodium: 561 mg

Dietary Exchanges: 3 Meat, 3 Starch

Layered Taco Salad 🌾

Remake a restaurant classic with lean ground beef, fat-free sour cream, and low-fat cheese.

½ pound 95% lean ground beef

1½ teaspoons chili powder

1½ teaspoons ground cumin, divided

½ cup picante sauce

1 teaspoon sugar

6 cups shredded romaine lettuce

2 plum tomatoes, seeded and diced

½ cup chopped green onions

¼ cup chopped fresh cilantro

28 crumbled nacho-flavored baked tortilla chips (2 ounces)

½ cup fat-free sour cream

½ cup (2 ounces) shredded reduced-fat sharp Cheddar or Mexican blend cheese

1. Coat large skillet with nonstick cooking spray and heat over medium-high heat. Brown beef 3 to 5 minutes, stirring to break up meat. Drain fat. Stir in chili powder and 1 teaspoon cumin. Let cool.

2. Combine picante sauce, sugar and remaining ½ teaspoon cumin in small bowl.

3. To assemble, place lettuce in 11×7-inch casserole. Layer with beef, tomatoes, green onions, cilantro and chips. Top with sour cream; sprinkle with cheese. Spoon picante sauce mixture on top.

MAKES 4 SERVINGS
(ABOUT 2 CUPS PER SERVING)

Calories: 258, Total Fat: 9 g, Saturated Fat: 4 g, Protein: 21 g, Carbohydrate: 25 g, Cholesterol: 46 mg, Fiber: 5 g, Sodium: 555 mg

Dietary Exchanges: ½ Fat, 2 Meat, 1 Starch, 2 Vegetable

Mediterranean Sandwiches

Chicken tenders, which are the lean, tender strips under the breast of the chicken, make these sandwiches lower in fat than most.

1¼ pounds chicken tenders, cut crosswise in half

1 large tomato, cut into bite-size pieces

½ small cucumber, halved lengthwise, seeded and sliced

½ cup sweet onion slices (about 1 small)

2 tablespoons cider vinegar

1 tablespoon olive oil or canola oil

3 teaspoons minced fresh oregano or ½ teaspoon dried oregano

2 teaspoons minced fresh mint or ¼ teaspoon dried mint

¼ teaspoon salt

6 (6-inch) whole wheat pita bread rounds

12 lettuce leaves (optional)

1. Coat large skillet with nonstick cooking spray and heat over medium heat. Add chicken; cook and stir 7 to 10 minutes or until browned and cooked through. Cool slightly.

2. Combine chicken, tomato, cucumber and onion in medium bowl. Drizzle with vinegar and oil; toss to coat. Sprinkle with oregano, mint and salt; toss to combine.

3. Cut pitas in half crosswise; gently open. Place 1 lettuce leaf in each pita bread half, if desired. Divide chicken mixture evenly among pita bread halves.

MAKES 6 SERVINGS
(2 FILLED PITA HALVES PER SERVING)

Calories: 242, Total Fat: 6 g, Saturated Fat: 1 g, Protein: 23 g, Carbohydrate: 24 g, Cholesterol: 50 mg, Fiber: 2 g, Sodium: 353 mg

Dietary Exchanges: 2½ Meat, 1½ Starch

Cream-Cheesy Garden Chowder

Instead of heavy cream, reduced-fat cream cheese lightens up this cheesy soup.

1 can (about 14 ounces) fat-free chicken broth

2 cups frozen corn

2 cups frozen diced hash brown potatoes

8 ounces frozen chopped green bell peppers

½ teaspoon dried thyme

1 teaspoon seafood seasoning

⅛ teaspoon red pepper flakes (optional)

½ cup fat-free (skim) milk

2 ounces reduced-fat cream cheese, cut into small pieces

¼ teaspoon salt (optional)

Dash black pepper

1. Bring broth to a boil in large saucepan over high heat. Add corn, hash browns, bell peppers, thyme, seafood seasoning and red pepper, if desired. Return to a boil. Reduce heat. Cover. Simmer 15 minutes or until peppers are tender.

2. Remove from heat. Whisk in milk, cream cheese, salt, if desired, and black pepper until cheese melts. Let stand 5 minutes before serving.

MAKES 4 SERVINGS
(1¼ CUPS PER SERVING)

Calories: 209, Total Fat: 3 g, Saturated Fat: 2 g, Protein: 8 g, Carbohydrate: 40 g, Cholesterol: 7 mg, Fiber: 5 g, Sodium: 548 mg

Dietary Exchanges: ½ Fat, 2½ Starch

Stuffed Eggplant ▾CARB

Sirloin is one of the leanest cuts of beef and makes this a filling low-carbohydrate meal.

2 eggplants (about 8 to 12 ounces each), halved lengthwise

1 teaspoon salt

1½ teaspoons chopped garlic

1 teaspoon black pepper

1 pound boneless beef sirloin steak, trimmed of visible fat and cut into ¼-inch strips

2 cups sliced red and green bell peppers

2 cups sliced mushrooms

¼ cup water

Pinch paprika

Chopped fresh parsley

MAKES 4 SERVINGS
(1 STUFFED EGGPLANT HALF PER SERVING)

Calories: 195
Total Fat: 5 g
Saturated Fat: 2 g
Protein: 25 g
Carbohydrate: 12 g
Cholesterol: 42 mg
Fiber: 4 g
Sodium: 348 mg

Dietary Exchanges:
2½ Meat, 2½ Vegetable

1. Preheat oven to 450°F. Coat baking dish with nonstick cooking spray.

2. Place eggplant halves face-up in large baking dish. Pierce cut sides with fork in approximately 8 places. Sprinkle each eggplant half with ¼ teaspoon salt. Cover with foil; bake 45 minutes.

3. Meanwhile, coat large skillet with nonstick cooking spray. Add garlic and black pepper; cook over medium heat 2 minutes, stirring lightly. Add sirloin strips; cook and stir 5 minutes.

4. Add bell peppers; cook 5 minutes. Add mushrooms; cook 5 minutes. Add water; stir and cover. Remove skillet from heat.

5. Remove eggplant from oven, let cool 5 minutes. Mash cooked eggplant centers with fork, but do not break shells.

6. Top each half with one fourth beef mixture; blend with mashed eggplant. Cover with foil; bake 15 minutes. Remove from oven. Garnish with paprika and parsley.

Butternut Squash Soup ⬇

Fat-free half-and-half makes this a low-fat yet rich soup.

2 teaspoons olive oil

1 large sweet onion, chopped

1 medium red bell pepper, chopped

2 packages (10 ounces each) frozen puréed butternut squash, thawed

1 can (10¾ ounces) condensed reduced-sodium chicken broth, undiluted

¼ teaspoon ground nutmeg

⅛ teaspoon white pepper

½ cup fat-free half-and-half

1. Heat oil in large saucepan over medium-high heat. Add onion and bell pepper; cook 5 minutes, stirring occasionally. Add squash, broth, nutmeg and white pepper; bring to a boil over high heat. Reduce heat; cover and simmer about 15 minutes or until vegetables are very tender.

2. Purée soup in saucepan with hand-held immersion blender or in batches in food processor or blender. Return soup to saucepan.

3. Stir in half-and-half; heat through. Add additional half-and-half, if necessary, to thin soup to desired consistency.

Note: Butternut squash is a type of winter squash, and it's an excellent source of beta-carotene. It's also a very good source of vitamin C, potassium, and dietary fiber.

MAKES 4 SERVINGS
(1½ CUPS PER SERVING)

Calories: 152
Total Fat: 3 g
Saturated Fat: 1 g
Protein: 6 g
Carbohydrate: 28 g
Cholesterol: 13 mg
Fiber: 3 g
Sodium: 155 mg

Dietary Exchanges:
½ Fat, 2 Starch

Grilled Portobello and Spring Green Sandwiches

Portobello mushrooms are low in fat, high in fiber, and replace meat in this sandwich.

MARINADE

2 tablespoons extra-virgin olive oil

1½ tablespoons balsamic vinegar

1 tablespoon water

1 tablespoon coarse-grain Dijon mustard

1 teaspoon dried oregano

1 clove garlic, minced

¼ teaspoon salt

½ teaspoon black pepper

4 large portobello mushroom caps, wiped with damp towel, gills and stems removed

8 slices (8 ounces) Italian bread

Nonstick cooking spray

¼ cup (1 ounce) crumbled reduced-fat blue cheese

2 to 3 ounces spring greens

1. Combine all marinade ingredients in medium bowl. Place mushrooms on sheet of foil or large serving platter. Brush 2 tablespoons marinade evenly over mushrooms; set aside remaining marinade. Let mushrooms stand 30 minutes.

2. Coat grill pan with nonstick cooking spray and place over medium-high heat. Coat both sides of bread pieces with nonstick cooking spray, grill bread 1 minute on each side, pressing down with flat spatula to flatten slightly. Place on individual dinner plates and set aside.

3. Grill mushrooms 3 to 4 minutes, turn and grill 3 to 4 minutes more or until beginning to brown. Place on top of bread slices. Sprinkle evenly with blue cheese.

4. Combine spring greens with reserved marinade, tossing gently, yet thoroughly to coat. Pile equal amounts of spring greens on top of mushrooms and serve between bread slices.

MAKES 4 SERVINGS
(1 SANDWICH PER SERVING)

Calories: 275, Total Fat: 10 g, Saturated Fat: 2 g, Protein: 9 g, Carbohydrate: 36 g, Cholesterol: 4 mg, Fiber: 3 g, Sodium: 590 mg

Dietary Exchanges: 2 Fat, 2 Starch, 1 Vegetable

Sirloin Steak Antipasto Salad

Using fat-free, reduced-sodium salad dressing saves plenty of calories, fat, and sodium.

3 cloves garlic, minced

½ teaspoon black pepper

1 boneless beef top sirloin steak (about 1 pound and ¾ inch thick), trimmed of fat

8 cups torn romaine lettuce

16 cherry tomatoes, halved

16 pitted kalamata olives, halved lengthwise

1 can (14 ounces) quartered artichoke hearts in water, rinsed and drained

⅓ cup fat-free reduced-sodium Italian or Caesar salad dressing

¼ cup fresh basil, cut into thin strips

1. Prepare grill for direct cooking or preheat broiler. Sprinkle garlic and pepper over steak. Grill over medium-hot coals or broil 4 inches from heat 4 minutes per side for medium-rare doneness or until desired doneness. Transfer steak to carving board. Tent with foil. Let stand at least 5 minutes.

2. Meanwhile, combine romaine, tomatoes, olives and artichoke hearts in large bowl. Add dressing; toss well. Transfer to 4 plates. Carve steak crosswise into thin slices; arrange over salads. Drizzle juices from carving board over steak. Sprinkle basil over salads.

MAKES 4 SERVINGS

Calories: 250, Total Fat: 7 g, Saturated Fat: 2 g, Protein: 30 g, Carbohydrate: 21 g, Cholesterol: 53 mg, Fiber: 9 g, Sodium: 776 mg

Dietary Exchanges: 3 Meat, 1 Starch, 1 Vegetable

Barley and Sausage Gumbo 🌾
Replacing rice with barley adds fiber, vitamins, and whole grains.

1 small onion, chopped

1 large green bell pepper, chopped

1 cup frozen sliced okra

1 medium stalk celery, chopped

1 clove garlic, minced

1 cup reduced-sodium chicken broth

1 cup no-salt-added tomato purée

¼ cup uncooked pearl barley

1 teaspoon dried oregano

¼ teaspoon salt (optional)

⅛ teaspoon red pepper flakes

2 low-fat chicken andouille sausages (3 ounces each), sliced ½ inch thick

Slow Cooker Directions

1. Place onion, bell pepper, okra, celery and garlic in slow cooker. Add chicken broth, tomato purée, barley, oregano, salt, if desired, and red pepper flakes; stir. Add sliced sausages. Cover; cook on LOW 5 to 6 hours.

2. Let stand 5 minutes before serving.

MAKES 4 SERVINGS
(1⅓ CUPS PER SERVING)

Calories: 175, Total Fat: 5 g, Saturated Fat: 1 g, Protein: 12 g, Carbohydrate: 24 g, Cholesterol: 31 mg, Fiber: 6 g, Sodium: 363 mg

Dietary Exchanges: 1 Meat, 1½ Starch

Salmon Black Bean Patties `CARB`

An egg white replaces mayonnaise in this healthy and quick meal.

1 can (7½ ounces) pink salmon, drained

½ cup no-salt-added black beans, rinsed and drained

¼ cup dry bread crumbs

¼ cup sliced green onions

1 egg white

1 tablespoon chopped fresh cilantro

1 tablespoon lime juice

Pinch ground red pepper or seafood seasoning mix, to taste

Black pepper

1 tablespoon canola oil

1. Place salmon in medium mixing bowl; shred with fork.

2. Add beans, bread crumbs, green onions, egg white, cilantro, lime juice, red pepper and black pepper to bowl. Shape mixture into 3 patties about 1¼ inches thick. Refrigerate 30 minutes or until ready to cook.

3. Heat oil in large skillet over medium heat. Add patties and cook 2 to 3 minutes on each side or until golden brown.

Note: The bones and skin in the salmon can are edible and a good source of calcium and beneficial omega-3 fats.

Serving suggestion: Serve with grilled eggplant slices or whole grain hamburger buns and your favorite salsa, if your diet permits.

**MAKES
3 SERVINGS
(1 PATTY PER
SERVING**

Calories: 205
Total Fat: 10 g
Saturated Fat: 2 g
Protein: 16 g
Carbohydrate: 13 g
Cholesterol: 16 mg
Fiber: 3 g
Sodium: 504 mg

Dietary Exchanges:
1 Fat, 2 Meat, 1 Starch

Swiss, Tomato and Turkey Patty Melt [CARB]

*With or without a bun, this classic recipe is lighter
due to lean ground turkey and low-fat cheese.*

**1 pound lean ground
turkey**

**½ packet (0.4 ounce) ranch
salad dressing mix**

**1 medium green onion,
finely chopped (green
and white parts)**

1 teaspoon olive oil

**2 slices reduced-fat
Swiss cheese, halved
diagonally**

1 medium tomato, diced

**Whole-grain bread
or hamburger buns
(optional)**

1. Combine turkey, salad dressing mix and green onion in medium bowl. Mix well. Shape into 4 patties.

2. Heat large skillet over medium heat. Coat skillet with nonstick cooking spray. Add oil; tilt skillet to coat bottom evenly. Add patties. Cook 14 minutes or until cooked through (165°F), turning once.

3. Remove skillet from heat. Top each patty with cheese. Cover. Let stand 2 to 3 minutes or until cheese melts. Top each patty with tomatoes. Serve with buns, if desired.

Note: Adding whole-grain hamburger buns to this meal would add 110 calories, 2 g fat, <1g saturated fat, 6 g protein, 23 g carbohydrate, 0 g cholesterol, 4 g fiber, and 240 mg sodium.

**MAKES
4 SERVINGS**
(1 PATTY PER
SERVING)

Calories: 239
Total Fat: 11 g
Saturated Fat: 3 g
Protein: 28 g
Carbohydrate: 3 g
Cholesterol: 75 mg
Fiber: <1 g
Sodium: 253 mg

Dietary Exchanges:
4 Meat

Blueberry-Almond Waldorf Salad

A fresh and low-sodium dressing keeps this salad light.

¼ cup sliced almonds

¼ cup plain low-fat yogurt

1 teaspoon honey

½ teaspoon whole-grain or regular Dijon mustard

1 large Gala or other red apple, halved, cored and cut into ½-inch pieces

1 large Granny Smith or Golden Delicious apple, halved, cored and cut into ½-inch pieces

½ cup fresh blueberries

2 cups baby spinach

MAKES 4 SERVINGS
(1 CUP PER SERVING)

Calories: 107
Total Fat: 3 g
Saturated Fat: <1 g
Protein: 3 g
Carbohydrate: 19 g
Cholesterol: 1 mg
Fiber: 4 g
Sodium: 34 mg

Dietary Exchanges:
½ Fat, 1½ Fruit

1. Place almonds in small nonstick skillet over medium-low heat. Cook 3 to 4 minutes until lightly toasted, stirring frequently. Transfer to plate to cool.

2. Stir yogurt, honey, and mustard in large bowl until smooth. Add apples, blueberries, spinach and almonds; toss to coat. Serve immediately.

Note: This recipe is loaded with nutritional value. Blueberries are packed with antioxidants and fiber. Almonds are known for their vitamin E content, monounsaturated fats, and ability to lower after-meal rises in blood sugar. Spinach is filled with antioxidants that act as anti-cancer agents.

Chicken, Hummus and Vegetable Wraps

Packed with fiber, hummus is a low-fat replacement for mayonnaise or a greasy sauce.

¾ cup hummus (regular, roasted red pepper or roasted garlic)

4 (8- to 10-inch) sun-dried tomato or spinach wraps or whole wheat tortillas

2 cups chopped cooked chicken breast

Chipotle hot pepper sauce or Louisiana-style hot pepper sauce (optional)

½ cup shredded carrots

½ cup chopped unpeeled cucumber

½ cup thinly sliced radishes

2 tablespoons chopped fresh mint or basil

Spread hummus evenly over wraps all the way to edges. Arrange chicken over hummus; sprinkle with hot sauce, if desired. Top with carrots, cucumber, radishes and mint. Roll up tightly. Cut in half diagonally.

Variation: Substitute alfalfa sprouts for the radishes. For tasty appetizers, cut wraps into bite-size pieces.

MAKES 4 SERVINGS
(1 WRAP PER SERVING)

Calories: 308, Total Fat: 10 g, Saturated Fat: 1 g, Protein: 32 g, Carbohydrate: 32 g, Cholesterol: 60 mg, Fiber: 15 g, Sodium: 540 mg

Dietary Exchanges: 3 Meat, 2 Starch

Open-Faced Egg Salad Sandwiches

Lose the top slice of bread to make a low-carbohydrate and low-fat classic sandwich.

6 hard-cooked eggs

3 tablespoons reduced-fat mayonnaise

½ cup finely chopped green onions

1½ tablespoons sweet pickle relish

¼ to ½ teaspoon celery seed

¼ teaspoon salt

⅛ teaspoon black pepper

4 slices reduced-calorie, high-fiber bread

2 cups packed spring greens

1. Separate egg yolks from whites; discard 4 yolks or reserve for another use.

2. Combine remaining 2 egg yolks and mayonnaise in medium bowl; mix well. Finely chop egg whites and add to mixture. Stir in green onions, pickle relish, celery seed, salt and pepper; mix well.

3. Top each bread slice evenly with greens and egg salad.

Tip: To prepare hard-cooked eggs, place the eggs in a single layer in a saucepan. Add cold water to cover the eggs by 1 inch; cover and bring to a boil over high heat. Remove from the heat and let stand 15 minutes. Immediately pour off the water, cover with cold water and let stand until the eggs have cooled.

MAKES 4 SERVINGS

Calories: 104, Total Fat: 3 g, Saturated Fat: <1 g, Protein: 9 g, Carbohydrate: 14 g, Cholesterol: 104 mg, Fiber: 6 g, Sodium: 400 mg

Dietary Exchanges: 1 Meat, 1 Starch

Spinach and Sausage Pizza

In place of heavy cheese and fatty meats, this pizza is loaded with veggies and turkey sausage for less fat and calories.

3 ounces (1 link) smoked turkey sausage, thinly sliced

2 ready-made whole wheat pizza crusts (5 ounces each)

½ cup fat-free ricotta cheese

1 clove garlic, crushed

½ teaspoon Italian seasoning

2 tablespoons grated Parmesan cheese

2 cups baby spinach leaves, coarsely chopped

2 plum tomatoes, thinly sliced

½ cup (2 ounces) shredded reduced-fat mozzarella cheese

1. Coat small skillet with nonstick cooking spray and heat over medium heat. Add turkey slices and cook until browned. Set aside.

2. Preheat oven to 450°F. Place pizza crusts on baking sheet.

3. Combine ricotta cheese, garlic, Italian seasoning and Parmesan cheese in small bowl. Spread in thin layer over pizza crusts within ½ inch of edge. Layer sausage evenly over cheese mixture.

4. Sprinkle spinach over sausage. Arrange tomatoes on top and layer with mozzarella cheese. Bake 12 to 15 minutes or until cheese is melted and golden brown and edges are crisp. Slice each pizza into 6 slices.

MAKES 6 SERVINGS
(2 SLICES PER SERVING)

Calories: 210, Total Fat: 6 g, Saturated Fat: 3 g, Protein: 12 g, Carbohydrate: 28 g, Cholesterol: 20 mg, Fiber: 5 g, Sodium: 525 mg

Dietary Exchanges: 1 Meat, 2 Starch

Sweet Surprises

Multigrain White Chocolate Cranberry Cookies

Whole wheat flour retains more nutrients and fiber than white flour.

- **2 cups whole wheat flour**
- **1½ cups uncooked 5-grain cereal***
- **1 teaspoon baking soda**
- **½ teaspoon salt**
- **¾ cup canola oil**
- **¾ cup packed brown sugar**
- **⅓ cup granulated sugar**
- **2 eggs**
- **1 tablespoon vanilla**
- **1 cup dried cranberries**
- **½ cup white chocolate chips**

*5-grain cereal is a combination of oats, wheat, rye, barley, flaxseed, and triticale. If unavailable, you may substitute with oatmeal.

1. Preheat oven to 375°F. Combine flour, cereal, baking soda and salt in medium bowl.

2. Combine oil, brown sugar, granulated sugar, eggs and vanilla in large bowl. Add flour mixture; stir to combine. Stir in cranberries and chips. Drop dough by rounded teaspoonfuls onto ungreased cookie sheets.

3. Bake 8 to 10 minutes or until golden brown but soft in center. Cool 1 minute on cookie sheets. Remove to wire racks; cool completely.

MAKES 36 SERVINGS
(2 COOKIES PER SERVING)

Calories: 124, Total Fat: 6 g, Saturated Fat: 1 g, Protein: 2 g, Carbohydrate: 17 g, Cholesterol: 12 mg, Fiber: 1 g, Sodium: 107 mg

Dietary Exchanges: 1 Fat, 1 Starch

Café Mocha Cupcakes

Reduced-fat, sugar-free whipped topping is as tasty as high-calorie frosting.

2 tablespoons plus
    2 teaspoons instant
    espresso coffee
    powder, divided

1⅓ cups plus 1 tablespoon
    water, divided

1 package (about
    18 ounces) devil's food
    cake mix

3 eggs

⅓ cup canola oil

1 container (8 ounces)
    reduced-fat sugar-free
    whipped topping

Cocoa powder
    (optional)

1. Preheat oven to 350°F. Line 24 standard (2½-inch) muffin cups with paper baking cups.

2. Dissolve 2 tablespoons coffee powder in 1⅓ cups water in large bowl. Add cake mix, eggs and oil; beat with electric mixer at low speed 30 seconds. Beat at medium speed 2 minutes, scraping bowl occasionally. Pour batter evenly into prepared muffin cups.

3. Bake 17 to 22 minutes or until toothpick inserted into centers comes out clean. Remove cupcakes from pan; cool completely on wire racks.

4. Dissolve remaining 2 teaspoons coffee powder in 1 tablespoon water in small cup. Fold coffee mixture into whipped topping until well blended. Spread frosting over cupcakes; sprinkle with cocoa powder, if desired. Serve immediately or cover and refrigerate until ready to serve.

**MAKES
24 SERVINGS**
(1 CUPCAKE PER
SERVING)

Calories: 150
Total Fat: 8 g
Saturated Fat: 2 g
Protein: 2 g
Carbohydrate: 19 g
Cholesterol: 26 mg
Fiber: 1 g
Sodium: 187 mg

Dietary Exchanges:
1 Fat, 1 Starch

Coconut Cream Pie Bowls

A simple way to keep calories low is to skip a pie crust and serve this dessert in a bowl.

2 cups fat-free (skim) milk

¼ cup sugar

3 tablespoons cornstarch

⅛ teaspoon salt

¼ cup cholesterol-free egg substitute

¾ cup shredded coconut

1 tablespoon reduced-fat margarine

1 teaspoon vanilla

1 teaspoon coconut extract

¾ cup fat-free whipped topping

1. Combine milk, sugar, cornstarch and salt in medium saucepan. Whisk until well blended and cornstarch is dissolved. Cook over medium heat, stirring constantly, until mixture thickens and begins to boil. Boil 1 minute; remove from heat.

2. Whisk 2 tablespoons milk mixture into egg substitute in small bowl until well blended. Slowly pour mixture back into saucepan, stirring rapidly to avoid lumps. Cook, stirring constantly, over medium heat 5 minutes until mixture thickens. Remove from heat.

3. Stir in coconut, margarine, vanilla and coconut extract. Pour into 6 (6-ounce) ramekins; chill. Top with whipped topping before serving.

MAKES 6 SERVINGS
(1 RAMEKIN PLUS 2 TABLESPOONS WHIPPED TOPPING PER SERVING)

Calories: 143
Total Fat: 4 g
Saturated Fat: 3 g
Protein: 4 g
Carbohydrate: 21 g
Cholesterol: 2 mg
Fiber: 1 g
Sodium: 132 mg

Dietary Exchanges:
1 Fat, 1½ Starch

Double Chocolate Cupcakes

Unsweetened cocoa powder is low in calories but intense in flavor.

1 cup all-purpose flour

½ cup unsweetened cocoa powder

1 teaspoon baking soda

¼ teaspoon salt

¾ cup granulated sugar

3 tablespoons stick margarine, softened

½ cup cholesterol-free egg substitute

1 teaspoon vanilla

½ cup reduced-fat buttermilk

2 tablespoons miniature semisweet chocolate chips

2 tablespoons powdered sugar

1. Preheat oven to 350°F. Line 12 standard (2½-inch) muffin cups with paper baking cups.

2. Combine flour, cocoa, baking soda and salt in medium bowl. Beat granulated sugar and margarine in large bowl with electric mixer at medium speed until well blended. Add egg substitute and vanilla; beat until blended. (Batter will be thin.) Alternately add flour mixture and buttermilk, beating until just combined after each addition. Stir in chocolate chips. Spoon batter evenly into prepared muffin cups.

3. Bake about 15 minutes or until toothpick inserted into centers comes out clean. Cool in pan 5 minutes. Transfer to wire rack to cool completely.

4. Sprinkle with powdered sugar just before serving.

MAKES 12 SERVINGS
(1 CUPCAKE PER SERVING)

Calories: 143
Total Fat: 3 g
Saturated Fat: 1 g
Protein: 3 g
Carbohydrate: 25 g
Cholesterol: <1 mg
Fiber: 1 g
Sodium: 213 mg

Dietary Exchanges:
½ Fat, 1½ Starch

Cool Gelatin Dessert

Reduced-fat sour cream adds a creamy finish to a low-carbohydrate summertime treat.

2 cups water

1 package (4-serving size) sugar-free strawberry gelatin

1 pound (16 ounces) fresh strawberries or thawed frozen unsweetened strawberries

3 mashed bananas

1 can (16 ounces) crushed pineapple in juice, drained

1 pint reduced-fat sour cream

Mint (optional)

MAKES 12 SERVINGS

Calories: 108
Total Fat: 5 g
Saturated Fat: 3 g
Protein: 2 g
Carbohydrate: 15 g
Cholesterol: 16 mg
Dietary Fiber: 2 g
Sodium: 37 mg

Dietary Exchanges:
1 Fat, 1 Fruit

1. Bring water to a boil in large pot. Add gelatin; stir until gelatin completely dissolves. Add strawberries, bananas and pineapple; stir gently until well combined.

2. Remove from heat and pour into an 8-inch square pan and refrigerate 4 hours or until firm. Cut into 12 squares. Top with dollop of sour cream and garnish with mint, if desired, before serving.

Tip: Instead of reduced-fat sour cream, you may also top with a dollop of reduced-fat vanilla yogurt.

Chocolate Spice Bundt Cake with Orange Glaze

Egg substitute helps to reduce fat and cholesterol while maintaining taste and texture.

1 package
   (about 18 ounces)
   devil's food cake mix

1⅓ cups water

¾ cup cholesterol-free egg
   substitute

2 tablespoons canola oil

1 tablespoon instant
   coffee granules

1 tablespoon grated
   orange peel

1 teaspoon ground
   cinnamon

½ cup orange juice

1 teaspoon cornstarch

1. Preheat oven to 325°F. Coat bundt pan with nonstick cooking spray.

2. Beat cake mix, water, egg substitute, oil, coffee, orange peel and cinnamon in large bowl with electric mixer at medium speed until well blended. Pour batter into prepared pan. Bake 35 to 37 minutes or until toothpick inserted near center comes out clean. Cool in pan on wire rack 10 minutes. Invert onto wire rack; cool completely.

3. Combine orange juice and cornstarch in small saucepan; stir until cornstarch is dissolved. Bring to a boil over medium-high heat. Boil 1 minute or until thickened. Remove from heat; cool completely. Spoon over cake.

Variation: For deeper coffee flavor, add additional 1 tablespoon of coffee granules to cake batter.

**MAKES
16 SERVINGS**

Calories: 164
Total Fat: 7 g
Saturated Fat: 1 g
Protein: 3 g
Carbohydrate: 25 g
Cholesterol: 0 mg
Fiber: 1 g
Sodium: 289 mg

Dietary Exchanges:
1½ Fat, 1½ Starch

Melon Cup

A small amount of granola topping keeps this treat healthy and fresh without adding too much fat.

2 cups cubed watermelon (or any melon of your choice)

3 cups vanilla low-fat yogurt

½ cup natural granola

Place melon in bottom of 4 dessert cups. Add yogurt and top with granola.

MAKES 4 SERVINGS

Calories: 234, Total Fat: 4 g, Saturated Fat: 3 g, Protein: 11 g, Carbohydrate: 40 g, Cholesterol: 9 mg, Dietary Fiber: 1 g, Sodium: 128 mg

Dietary Exchanges: 1 Fat, 1 Milk, 1½ Starch

Angelic Cupcakes

Angel food cake mix is fat-free, but still makes moist and delicious cupcakes.

1 package (about 16 ounces) angel food cake mix

1¼ cups cold water

¼ teaspoon peppermint extract (optional)

9 drops red food coloring

4½ cups light whipped topping

MAKES 36 SERVINGS
(1 CUPCAKE PER SERVING)

Calories: 68
Total Fat: 1 g
Saturated Fat: 1 g
Protein: 1 g
Carbohydrate: 13 g
Cholesterol: 0 mg
Fiber: 0 g
Sodium: 113 mg

Dietary Exchanges:
1 Starch

1. Preheat oven to 375°F. Line 36 standard (2½-inch) muffin cups with paper baking cups.

2. Beat cake mix, water and peppermint extract, if desired, in large bowl with electric mixer at low speed 2 minutes. Pour half of batter into medium bowl; fold in 9 drops red food coloring. Alternate spoonfuls of white and pink batter in each prepared muffin cup, filling three-fourths full.

3. Bake 11 minutes or until cupcakes are golden brown with deep cracks on top. Remove to wire racks; cool completely.

4. Divide whipped topping between 2 small bowls. Add 2 drops red food coloring to 1 bowl; stir gently until whipped topping is evenly colored. Frost cupcakes with pink and white whipped topping as desired.

Pink Peppermint Meringues

Meringues are typically fat-free, however sugar-free peppermints make these almost carbohydrate-free as well.

3 egg whites

⅛ teaspoon peppermint extract

5 drops red food coloring

½ cup superfine sugar*

6 sugar-free peppermint candies, finely crushed

Or use ½ cup granulated sugar processed in food processor 1 minute until very fine.

MAKES ABOUT 6 DOZEN SERVINGS
(1 MERINGUE PER SERVING)

Calories: 6
Total Fat: <1 g
Saturated Fat: 0 g
Protein: <1 g
Carbohydrate: 2 g
Cholesterol: 0 mg
Fiber: 0 g
Sodium: 3 mg

Dietary Exchanges:
Free

1. Preheat oven to 200°F. Line cookie sheets with parchment paper.

2. Beat egg whites in medium bowl with electric mixer at medium-high speed 45 seconds or until frothy. Beat in peppermint extract and food coloring. Add sugar, 1 tablespoon at a time, while mixer is running. Beat until egg whites are stiff and glossy.

3. Drop meringue by teaspoonfuls into 1-inch mounds on prepared cookie sheets; sprinkle evenly with crushed candies.

4. Bake 2 hours or until meringues are dry when tapped. Transfer parchment paper with meringues to wire racks to cool completely.

No-Bake Cherry Cake

Sugar-free, fat-free instant pudding makes a fast and low-calorie filling.

1 (10-inch) prepared angel food cake

1½ cups fat-free (skim) milk

1 cup reduced-fat sour cream

1 package (4-serving size) vanilla fat-free sugar-free instant pudding and pie filling mix

1 can (21 ounces) light cherry pie filling

1. Tear cake into bite-sized pieces; press into 11×7-inch baking dish.

2. Beat milk, sour cream and pudding mix in medium bowl with wire whisk or electric mixer at medium speed 2 minutes or until thickened. Spread over cake in baking dish.

3. Spoon cherry pie filling evenly over top of cake. Chill before serving.

MAKES 12 SERVINGS

Calories: 156
Total Fat: 2 g
Saturated Fat: 1 g
Protein: 4 g
Carbohydrate: 31 g
Cholesterol: 7 mg
Fiber: 1 g
Sodium: 326 mg

Dietary Exchanges:
½ Meat, 1 Milk, 2 Starch

Shortcakes with Berries and Creamy Lemon Sauce

Replacing heavy cream with skim milk and reduced-fat whipped topping is a fast and easy fix.

BERRIES

½ **bag (1 pound) frozen unsweetened mixed berries, thawed, including any juices**

1 **tablespoon sugar substitute***

½ **teaspoon vanilla**

SAUCE

4 **ounces reduced-fat sugar-free whipped topping**

2 **tablespoons sugar substitute***

2 **tablespoons lemon juice**

2 **tablespoons fat-free (skim) milk**

SHORTCAKE

1½ **cups biscuit baking mix**

⅓ **cup fat-free (skim) milk**

2 **tablespoons sugar substitute***

½ **teaspoon grated lemon peel**

*This recipe was tested using sucralose-based sugar substitute.

MAKES 6 SERVINGS
(1 SHORTCAKE PER SERVING)

Calories: 191
Total Fat: 7 g
Saturated Fat: 3 g
Protein: 3 g
Carbohydrate: 33 g
Cholesterol: <1 mg
Fiber: 1 g
Sodium: 380 mg

Dietary Exchanges:
1½ Fat, 1 Fruit, 1 Starch

1. Preheat oven to 425°F. Coat baking sheet with nonstick cooking spray; set aside.

2. Combine berries with 1 tablespoon sugar substitute and vanilla in medium bowl; set aside. Combine sauce ingredients in separate medium bowl; mix well. Refrigerate.

3. Combine shortcake ingredients in separate medium bowl. Stir until just blended. Spoon batter onto prepared baking sheet in 6 equal mounds. Bake 10 minutes or until golden. Cool. Slice shortcakes in half crosswise. Place bottom half on serving plate. Top each with ⅓ cup berries, 2 tablespoons sauce and other half of shortcake.

Peanut Butter & Banana Cookies

Apple juice concentrate replaces pure sugar to reduce carbohydrates and calories.

¼ cup (½ stick) butter

½ cup mashed ripe banana

½ cup no-sugar-added natural peanut butter

¼ cup frozen unsweetened apple juice concentrate, thawed

1 egg

1 teaspoon vanilla

1 cup all-purpose flour

½ teaspoon baking soda

¼ teaspoon salt

½ cup chopped salted peanuts

Whole salted peanuts (optional)

1. Preheat oven to 375°F. Grease cookie sheets or lightly coat with nonstick cooking spray.

2. Beat butter in large bowl until creamy. Add banana and peanut butter; beat until smooth. Blend in apple juice concentrate, egg and vanilla. Beat in flour, baking soda and salt. Stir in chopped peanuts.

3. Drop dough by rounded tablespoonfuls 2 inches apart onto prepared cookie sheets; top each with 1 whole peanut, if desired.

4. Bake 8 minutes or until set. Cool completely on wire racks. Store in tightly covered container.

MAKES 24 SERVINGS
(1 COOKIE PER SERVING)

Calories: 100
Total Fat: 6 g
Saturated Fat: 2 g
Protein: 3 g
Carbohydrate: 9 g
Cholesterol: 14 mg
Fiber: 1 g
Sodium: 88 mg

Dietary Exchanges:
1½ Fat, ½ Starch

Enlightened Apple Crisp

Using low-fat granola as a topping dramatically cuts calories and fat.

2 tablespoons low-fat granola with almonds

1 red apple (8 ounces), such as Gala, diced into ½-inch pieces

1 tablespoon dried cranberries

¼ teaspoon apple pie spice or ground cinnamon

1 teaspoon reduced-fat margarine

1 packet sugar substitute*

¼ teaspoon almond extract

2 tablespoons vanilla low-fat ice cream

This recipe was tested using sucralose-based sugar substitute.

MAKES 2 SERVINGS

Calories: 150
Total Fat: 3 g
Saturated Fat: <1 g
Protein: 1 g
Carbohydrate: 32 g
Cholesterol: <1 mg
Fiber: 4 g
Sodium: 40 mg

Dietary Exchanges:
1 Fat, 1 Fruit, 1 Starch

1. Place granola in small resealable food storage bag. Crush lightly with rolling pin to form coarse crumbs; set aside.

2. Coat large skillet with nonstick cooking spray and heat over medium heat. Add apple, cranberries and apple pie spice; cook and stir 4 minutes or until apples are just tender.

3. Remove from heat; stir in margarine, sugar substitute and almond extract. Spoon ice cream into 2 dessert bowls or dessert plates; top with apple mixture and sprinkle with granola. Serve immediately.

Cream Cheese Brownie Royale

Reduced-fat cream cheese saves hundreds of calories without sacrificing flavor.

1 package (about 15 ounces) brownie mix for 8-inch square pan

⅔ cup cold coffee or water

1 package (8 ounces) reduced-fat cream cheese, softened

1 egg

5 teaspoons sugar substitute*

1 tablespoon fat-free (skim) milk

½ teaspoon vanilla

This recipe was tested using sucralose-based sugar substitute.

1. Preheat oven to 350°F. Coat 13×9-inch baking pan with nonstick cooking spray.

2. Combine brownie mix and coffee in large bowl; stir until blended. Spread brownie mixture evenly into prepared pan.

3. Beat cream cheese, egg, sugar substitute, milk and vanilla in medium bowl with electric mixer at medium speed until smooth. Spoon cream cheese mixture in small dollops over brownie mixture. Swirl cream cheese mixture into brownie mixture with tip of knife.

4. Bake 30 to 35 minutes or until toothpick inserted into center comes out clean. Cool completely in pan on wire rack.

5. Cover with foil and refrigerate 8 hours or until ready to serve. Cut into 16 squares. Garnish as desired.

MAKES 16 SERVINGS
(1 BROWNIE PER SERVING)

Calories: 167
Total Fat: 5 g
Saturated Fat: 2 g
Protein: 4 g
Carbohydrate: 28 g
Cholesterol: 7 mg
Fiber: 1 g
Sodium: 181 mg

Dietary Exchanges:
½ Fat, 2 Starch

Dreamy Orange Pie

Instead of a typical high-calorie pie filling, sugar-free ice cream and sherbet lighten things up.

8 whole reduced-fat honey graham crackers, crushed (1½ cups)

2 tablespoons reduced-fat margarine, melted

1 pint vanilla sugar-free ice cream, softened

1 pint orange sherbet, softened

10 tablespoons reduced-fat sugar-free whipped topping

10 mandarin orange slices

1. Preheat oven to 350°F. Coat 9-inch springform baking pan with nonstick cooking spray.

2. Combine graham cracker crumbs and margarine in medium bowl. Gently press crumb mixture on bottom and ½ inch up sides of pan. Bake 8 to 10 minutes or until lightly browned; cool completely on wire rack.

3. Spread ice cream evenly in cooled crust. Freeze 30 minutes or until firm to the touch. Spread orange sherbet evenly over ice cream; freeze at least 1 hour or until firm.

4. To serve, run knife carefully around edge of pan; remove side of pan. Cut into 10 slices. Top each slice with 1 tablespoon whipped topping and 1 orange slice.

MAKES
10 SERVINGS

Calories: 160
Total Fat: 4 g
Saturated Fat: 2 g
Protein: 3 g
Carbohydrate: 28 g
Cholesterol: 4 mg
Fiber: 2 g
Sodium: 139 mg

Dietary Exchanges:
2 Starch

Flourless Chocolate Cake

Using margarine instead of butter saves saturated fat and cholesterol.

3 squares (1 ounce each) semisweet chocolate, cut into large pieces

3 tablespoons margarine

1 tablespoon espresso powder or instant coffee granules

2 tablespoons hot water

4 eggs, separated

2 egg whites

⅔ cup sugar, divided

3 tablespoons unsweetened cocoa powder, sifted

1 teaspoon vanilla

½ teaspoon salt

Fat-free whipped topping (optional)

Fresh raspberries (optional)

MAKES 10 SERVINGS

Calories: 190
Total Fat: 8 g
Saturated Fat: 3 g
Protein: 4 g
Carbohydrate: 26 g
Cholesterol: 85 mg
Fiber: 1 g
Sodium: 240 mg

Dietary Exchanges:
1 Fat, 1½ Starch

1. Preheat oven to 300°F. Grease 9-inch springform pan; line bottom of pan with parchment paper.

2. Place chocolate and margarine in small heavy saucepan; heat over low heat, stirring frequently, until just melted. Remove from heat; set aside to cool. Dissolve espresso powder in hot water in small bowl.

3. Place 6 egg whites in large bowl. Beat egg yolks in medium bowl with electric mixer at high speed about 5 minutes or until pale yellow in color. Add ⅓ cup sugar; beat about 4 minutes or until mixture falls in ribbons from beaters. Slowly beat in melted chocolate mixture and espresso mixture at low speed until just blended. Beat in cocoa and vanilla until just blended.

4. Add salt to egg whites; beat at high speed about 2 minutes or until soft peaks form. Beat In remaining ⅓ cup sugar until stiff peaks form. Stir large spoonful of egg whites into chocolate mixture. Fold chocolate mixture into egg whites until almost blended. Spoon batter into prepared pan.

5. Bake 1 hour or until cake begins to pull away from side of pan. Cool on wire rack 10 minutes; run thin spatula around edge of cake. Carefully remove side of pan. Cool completely. Invert cake; remove bottom of pan and paper from cake. Cover and refrigerate at least 4 hours. Serve chilled with whipped topping and raspberries, if desired.

Fruit-Filled Cream Puffs

Although all oils have a lot of fat, canola oil is rich in heart-healthy fats.

1 cup water

⅓ cup canola oil

2 tablespoons sugar

¼ teaspoon salt

1 cup all-purpose flour

2 eggs

2 egg whites

1¾ cups fat-free (skim) milk

1 package (4-serving size) vanilla fat-free sugar-free instant pudding and pie filling mix

2 cups fresh berries, such as strawberries, raspberries or blueberries

**MAKES
10 SERVINGS**

Calories: 137
Total Fat: 8 g
Saturated Fat: 1 g
Protein: 3 g
Carbohydrate: 12 g
Cholesterol: 42 mg
Fiber: <1 g
Sodium: 83 mg

Dietary Exchanges:
1 Fat, 1 Starch

1. Preheat oven to 400°F. Coat large baking sheet with nonstick cooking spray or line with parchment paper.

2. Bring water, oil, sugar and salt to a boil in medium saucepan. Add flour all at once, stirring vigorously until dough pulls away from side of pan (about 1 minute). Immediately remove from heat; cool at least 5 minutes.

3. Add eggs and egg whites, 1 at a time, beating with spoon or whisk after each addition, until dough no longer looks slippery. Drop dough by scant ¼ cupfuls about 3 inches apart onto prepared baking sheet.

4. Bake 30 to 40 minutes or until dry and crisp. Remove to wire rack; cool completely. Meanwhile, whisk milk and pudding mix in medium bowl about 2 minutes or until thickened.

5. Cut off top third of each cream puff and pull out any strands of soft dough. Fill with pudding and berries; replace tops. Serve immediately or cover and refrigerate until ready to serve.

Banana Pudding Squares

Fat-free, sugar-free banana cream instant pudding and pie mix adds amazing flavor without excessive fat, carbohydrates, or calories.

1 cup graham cracker crumbs

2 tablespoons margarine, melted

1 package (8 ounces) fat-free cream cheese, softened

2 packages (4-serving size) banana cream fat-free sugar-free instant pudding and pie filling mix

3 cups fat-free (skim) milk

1 container (8 ounces) reduced-fat whipped topping, divided

2 medium bananas, peeled

1. Line 13×9-inch pan with foil and coat lightly with nonstick cooking spray. Stir graham cracker crumbs and margarine in small bowl until blended. Scatter crumbs into pan and press into even layer.

2. Beat cream cheese in large bowl with electric mixer at low speed until smooth. Add pudding mix and milk; beat at high speed 2 minutes or until smooth and creamy. Fold half of whipped topping into pudding until well blended. Reserve half of pudding mixture. Drop remaining pudding mixture by heaping tablespoonfuls onto crust. Gently spread into even layer.

3. Cut bananas in half lengthwise, then cut crosswise into ¼-inch slices. Sprinkle bananas evenly over pudding. Spoon reserved pudding mixture over bananas; spread into even layer.

4. Spread remaining whipped topping evenly over pudding mixture. Loosely cover with plastic wrap and refrigerate 2 hours (or up to 8 hours). Cut into squares.

MAKES 18 SERVINGS

Calories: 112
Total Fat: 4 g
Saturated Fat: 2 g
Protein: 4 g
Carbohydrate: 15 g
Cholesterol: 2 mg
Fiber: 1 g
Sodium: 292 mg

Dietary Exchanges:
½ Fat, 1 Starch

Cherry Cobbler

Frozen or fresh cherries, instead of canned cherries, make a healthier cobbler.

1 sheet frozen puff pastry, thawed

2 teaspoons fat-free (skim) milk

½ cup plus 1 teaspoon sucralose-sugar blend, divided

⅛ teaspoon plus ¼ teaspoon ground cinnamon, divided

1½ pounds frozen unsweetened tart or sweet cherries

3 tablespoons uncooked quick-cooking tapioca

1 teaspoon almond extract

2 tablespoons chilled margarine, cut into small pieces

Thawed fat-free whipped topping (optional)

1. Preheat oven to 400°F. Line baking sheet with parchment paper.

2. Unfold puff pastry sheet on lightly floured surface. Cut pastry into 10 shapes with 2½-inch scalloped cookie cutter; discard trimmings. Place cut-outs on prepared baking sheet; lightly brush with milk. Combine 1 teaspoon sucralose-sugar blend and ⅛ teaspoon cinnamon in small cup; sprinkle over cut-outs. Bake 12 to 15 minutes or until golden brown. Remove cut-outs to wire rack to cool completely.

3. Meanwhile, lightly spray 2-quart baking dish with nonstick cooking spray. Combine cherries, remaining ½ cup sucralose-sugar blend, tapioca, almond extract and remaining ¼ teaspoon cinnamon in large bowl. Mix well; let stand 15 minutes. Spoon cherry mixture into prepared baking dish; dot with margarine pieces.

4. Bake 40 to 45 minutes or until hot and bubbly. Cool 5 to 8 minutes. Spoon ⅓ cup cherry mixture into small dessert dish; top with pastry cut-out. Top each serving with whipped topping, if desired.

MAKES 10 SERVINGS
(1 PASTRY CUT-OUT AND ⅓ CUP CHERRY FILLING PER SERVING)

Calories: 184, Total Fat: 7 g, Saturated Fat: 2 g, Protein: 2 g, Carbohydrate: 26 g, Cholesterol: 0 mg, Fiber: 1 g, Sodium: 59 mg

Dietary Exchanges: 2 Starch

Mocha Cream Tartlets

These tartlets are low in carbohydrates thanks to sugar-free pudding and petite portion sizes.

- 1 package (4-serving size) cook-and-serve chocolate fat-free sugar-free pudding and pie filling mix
- 2 cups fat-free half-and-half, divided
- ⅛ teaspoon ground cinnamon
- 1½ teaspoons instant coffee granules
- ½ cup old-fashioned oats
- ½ cup all-purpose flour
- 1 tablespoon sugar
- ¼ cup graham cracker crumbs
- ¼ cup unsalted margarine, melted
- 1½ cups reduced-fat whipped topping
- 16 chocolate-covered espresso beans (optional)

1. Combine pudding mix and ½ cup half-and-half in medium saucepan; stir until smooth. Stir in remaining 1½ cups half-and-half, cinnamon and coffee; bring to a boil over medium-high heat, stirring constantly. Remove from heat; spoon into medium bowl and refrigerate at least 1 hour.

2. Preheat oven to 375°F. Line 16 standard (2½-inch) muffin cups with paper baking cups.

3. Combine oats, flour, sugar and graham cracker crumbs in medium bowl. Stir in margarine until mixture comes together when pressed. Spoon 1 tablespoon crumb mixture into each cup; press to form crust. Bake 13 minutes or until crusts are golden brown and firm. Cool completely in pan on wire rack.

4. To assemble tartlets, gently fold whipped topping into chocolate pudding. Spoon mixture into cooled crusts. Garnish with espresso beans, if desired.

Note: The filling in the tartlets may be soft or firm depending on the pudding mix. For a firmer filling, fold the whipped topping into the pudding, spoon it over the crusts, and chill for 2 or more hours.

**MAKES
16 SERVINGS**
(1 TARTLET PER SERVING)

Calories: 100
Total Fat: 5 g
Saturated Fat: 2 g
Protein: 2 g
Carbohydrate: 13 g
Cholesterol: 0 mg
Fiber: 0 g
Sodium: 70 mg

Dietary Exchanges:
1 Fat, 1 Starch

Peanut Crumb Cake

Reduced-fat peanut butter tastes virtually the same as regular peanut butter but with less fat and calories.

1 package (about 18 ounces) yellow cake mix

¾ cup reduced-fat peanut butter

¼ cup sucralose-brown sugar blend

1 cup water

¾ cup cholesterol-free egg substitute

¼ cup vegetable oil

⅓ cup mini semisweet chocolate chips

¼ cup peanut butter chips

¼ cup roasted peanuts, finely chopped

1. Preheat oven to 350°F. Lightly spray 13×9-inch baking pan with nonstick cooking spray.

2. Beat cake mix, peanut butter and brown sugar blend in large bowl with electric mixer at low speed until mixture resembles coarse crumbs. Remove ⅓ cup to medium bowl for topping. Add water, egg substitute and oil to remaining mixture; beat at medium speed until well blended.

3. Spread batter evenly in prepared pan. Add chocolate chips, peanut butter chips and peanuts to reserved crumb mixture; mix well. Sprinkle over batter.

4. Bake 38 to 42 minutes or until toothpick inserted into center comes out clean. Cool cake completely in pan on wire rack. Cut into 24 squares.

MAKES 24 SERVINGS

Calories: 203
Total Fat: 10 g
Saturated Fat: 2 g
Protein: 4 g
Carbohydrate: 25 g
Cholesterol: 0 mg
Fiber: 1 g
Sodium: 226 mg

Dietary Exchanges:
1½ Fat, 1½ Starch

Devil's Food Ice Cream Cake with Java Cream

Reduced-sugar devil's food cake mix has about half the sugar as regular devil's food cake mix.

1 package (about 18 ounces) reduced-sugar devil's food cake mix

1¼ cups plus 2 tablespoons water, divided

¾ cup cholesterol-free egg substitute

2 tablespoons canola oil

1½ tablespoons instant coffee granules

12 ounces fat-free whipped topping

3 cups vanilla fat-free ice cream, softened

1. Preheat oven to 350°F. Coat 2 (9-inch) cake pans with nonstick cooking spray.

2. Beat cake mix, 1¼ cups water, egg substitute and oil in large bowl with electric mixer at medium speed 2 minutes. Pour batter into prepared pans. Bake 20 to 25 minutes or until toothpick inserted into center comes out almost clean. Cool 10 minutes in pans on wire rack. Invert onto wire rack; cool completely.

3. Combine remaining 2 tablespoons water and coffee granules in medium bowl; stir until coffee is dissolved. Fold in whipped topping. Refrigerate until needed.

4. Place 1 cake layer on cake plate; spread evenly with ice cream and top with remaining cake layer. Frost sides and top of cake with whipped topping mixture. Freeze until ready to serve. Store leftovers in freezer.

Note: Bake 30 to 35 minutes if using 8-inch cake pans.

MAKES 18 SERVINGS

Calories: 195
Total Fat: 4 g
Saturated Fat: <1 g
Protein: 3 g
Carbohydrate: 36 g
Cholesterol: 0 mg
Fiber: <1 g
Sodium: 126 mg

Dietary Exchanges:
½ Fat, 2½ Starch

S'more Treats

Cocoa-flavored sweetened rice cereal is very low in fat to make these chocolatey treats.

2½ cups cocoa-flavored sweetened rice cereal

6 reduced-fat honey graham crackers

3 tablespoons margarine

1 tablespoon sucralose-brown sugar blend

3½ cups miniature marshmallows, divided

1 square (1 ounce) semisweet or milk chocolate, melted (optional)

1. Lightly spray 9-inch square baking pan with nonstick cooking spray. Place cereal in large bowl. Crumble graham crackers into ¼-inch pieces; add to bowl. Toss to combine.

2. Combine margarine and brown sugar blend in large microwavable bowl; microwave on HIGH 25 to 30 seconds or until melted. Add 2½ cups marshmallows to butter mixture; microwave on HIGH 1½ to 2 minutes, stirring after 1 minute, or until marshmallows are melted. Stir until mixture is smooth.

3. Add marshmallow mixture to cereal mixture; stir to coat. Add remaining 1 cup marshmallows; stir until blended. Press evenly into prepared pan using waxed paper. Cool completely. Drizzle with chocolate, if desired. Cut into 16 squares.

MAKES 16 SERVINGS
(1 SQUARE PER SERVING)

Calories: 89
Total Fat: 2 g
Saturated Fat: <1 g
Protein: <1 g
Carbohydrate: 16 g
Cholesterol: mg
Fiber: 0 g
Sodium: 79 mg

Dietary Exchanges:
1 Starch

Chocolate Peanut Butter Truffles

Reduced-fat peanut butter and rice cereal replace a typical fattening filling of whipping cream.

½ cup reduced-fat chunky peanut butter

3 tablespoons sugar substitute*

1 cup crisp rice cereal

3 tablespoons unsweetened cocoa powder

¼ cup mini semisweet chocolate chips

This recipe was tested using sucralose-based sugar substitute.

MAKES 5 SERVINGS
(4 TRUFFLES PER SERVING)

Calories: 220
Total Fat: 12 g
Saturated Fat: 3 g
Protein: 8 g
Carbohydrate: 25 g
Cholesterol: 0 mg
Fiber: 3 g
Sodium: 229 mg

Dietary Exchanges:
2 Fat, 1½ Starch

1. Place peanut butter in small microwavable bowl. Microwave on HIGH 10 seconds. Stir in sugar substitute with wooden spoon until smooth. Stir in cereal; mix well.

2. Line large plate with waxed paper. Spray hands with nonstick cooking spray and shape peanut butter mixture into 1-inch balls, pressing firmly. Place balls on prepared plate and freeze 15 minutes or up to 1 hour.

3. Spread cocoa on small plate. Roll each truffle in cocoa; return to large plate.

4. Place chocolate chips in small resealable food storage bag. Microwave on HIGH 10 seconds; knead bag. Repeat until chocolate is melted and smooth.

5. Press melted chocolate into one corner of bag; cut very small hole in corner. Drizzle chocolate over truffles. Let chocolate set before serving. Truffles can be refrigerated in airtight container up to 3 days.

No-Bake Red, White and Blue Cheesecake Cups

Reduced-fat and fat-free cream cheeses, along with reduced-fat sour cream, make a low-carbohydrate yet rich dessert.

¾ cup graham cracker crumbs (about 12 squares crushed)

⅓ cup plus 2 tablespoons sugar substitute*

4 tablespoons reduced-fat margarine, melted

8 ounces reduced-fat cream cheese

8 ounces fat-free cream cheese, room temperature

½ cup reduced-fat sour cream

1 cup reduced-fat whipped topping, divided

¼ teaspoon almond extract

6 medium strawberries, stemmed and halved

1 cup blueberries

This recipe was tested using sucralose-based sugar substitute.

1. Line 12 muffin cups with paper baking cups. Lightly spray cups with nonstick cooking spray.

2. Combine graham cracker crumbs, 2 tablespoons sugar substitute and margarine in medium bowl; mix well. Press 1 rounded tablespoon into bottom of each muffin cup. Place in refrigerator to chill.

3. Beat cream cheeses, ⅓ cup sugar substitute and sour cream in medium bowl with electric mixer at low speed until smooth. Beat in ½ cup whipped topping and almond extract. Fold in remaining whipped topping.

4. Spoon cheesecake filling over crusts; smooth tops. Place ½ strawberry in center of each cheesecake cup; arrange blueberries around strawberry. Refrigerate at least 2 hours or until set.

MAKES 12 SERVINGS

Calories: 139, Total Fat: 8 g, Saturated Fat: 3 g, Protein: 6 g, Carbohydrate: 12 g, Cholesterol: 15 mg, Fiber: 1 g, Sodium: 325 mg

Dietary Exchanges: 1½ Fat, 1 Starch

Tres Leches Cake

Sucralose-sugar blend adds sweetness for half the carbohydrates and calories as sugar.

1 package (about 18 ounces) reduced-sugar white cake mix

1¼ cups water

¾ cup cholesterol-free egg substitute

⅔ cup fat-free (skim) milk

½ cup reduced-fat sour cream

1 teaspoon vanilla

1 teaspoon sucralose-sugar blend

1 container (8 ounces) thawed fat-free whipped topping

½ teaspoon ground cinnamon (optional)

1. Preheat oven to 350°F. Lightly spray 13X9-inch pan with nonstick cooking spray.

2. Beat cake mix, water and egg substitute in large bowl with electric mixer at medium speed 2 to 3 minutes or until smooth. Spread batter evenly in prepared pan. Bake 30 to 33 minutes or until toothpick inserted into center comes out clean. Remove to wire rack; cool completely.

3. Poke holes in cake about 1½ inches deep and about ½ inch apart with wooden skewer.

4. Whisk milk, sour cream, vanilla and sucralose-sugar blend in medium bowl until smooth and well blended. Slowly pour over surface of cake, allowing cake to absorb mixture. Let cake stand 8 to 10 minutes or until milk mixture is completely absorbed. Cover and refrigerate.

5. Spread whipped topping evenly over cake. Lightly sprinkle with cinnamon, if desired. Cut into 24 squares and serve immediately. Cover and refrigerate any remaining cake.

MAKES 24 SERVINGS

Calories: 114
Total Fat: 2 g
Saturated Fat: <1 g
Protein: 2 g
Carbohydrate: 21 g
Cholesterol: 0 mg
Fiber: 0 g
Sodium: 81 mg

Dietary Exchanges:
1½ Starch

Chocolate Mousse Minis

Unsweetened cocoa powder intensifies the chocolate flavor and is low in calories and fat.

1 envelope unflavored gelatin

¼ cup water

¾ cup reduced-fat evaporated milk

1 egg yolk

⅓ cup unsweetened cocoa powder

⅓ cup semisweet chocolate chips

½ teaspoon vanilla

½ cup sugar substitute*

¾ cup plus 6 tablespoons reduced-fat whipped topping, divided

3 chocolate wafer cookies, crumbled

This recipe was tested using sucralose-based sugar substitute.

1. Sprinkle gelatin over water in medium saucepan. Let stand about 2 minutes or until gelatin softens. Whisk in evaporated milk, egg yolk and cocoa powder. Bring to a low simmer over medium heat; cook and stir 2 minutes, or until mixture is smooth and slightly thickened.

2. Remove from heat; whisk in chocolate chips, vanilla and sugar substitute until smooth. Transfer to medium bowl; let cool to room temperature, stirring every 5 minutes.

3. Fold in ¾ cup whipped topping and mix until smooth. Spoon about ¼ cup mousse into 6 (4-ounce) dessert glasses. Cover and refrigerate 1 hour.

4. To serve, top each glass with 1 tablespoon whipped topping and 1½ teaspoons cookie crumbs.

Note: Unsweetened cocoa powder has only 12 to 15 calories and 3 grams of carbohydrate per tablespoon. It also has 2 grams of heart-healthy fiber. It packs a chocolatey punch without ruining your diet.

MAKES 6 SERVINGS

Calories: 138
Total Fat: 7 g
Saturated Fat: 3 g
Protein: 5 g
Carbohydrate: 19 g
Cholesterol: 40 mg
Fiber: 2 g
Sodium: 58 mg

Dietary Exchanges:
1 Fat, 1 Starch

Orange Almond Cake ⬇

Almond paste replaces butter to make this low-fat and fresh cake.

⅔ cup all-purpose flour, plus additional for dusting pan

1 teaspoon baking powder

¼ teaspoon baking soda

¼ teaspoon salt

¾ cup granulated sugar

¼ cup almond paste

2 eggs

½ cup cholesterol-free egg substitute

2 teaspoons grated orange peel

1 teaspoon vanilla

2 teaspoons powdered sugar

Fresh berries (optional)

1. Preheat oven to 350°F. Cut circle of waxed paper or parchment paper to fit inside 9-inch round springform or cake pan. Coat pan with nonstick cooking spray. Place paper circle on bottom of pan; spray with cooking spray and dust with flour.

2. Combine ⅔ cup flour, baking powder, baking soda and salt in small bowl. Beat granulated sugar and almond paste in large bowl with electric mixer at medium speed until blended. Beat in eggs, egg substitute, orange peel and vanilla until smooth. Beat in flour mixture. Pour batter into prepared pan.

3. Bake 35 minutes or until toothpick inserted into center comes out with moist crumbs. Cool completely in pan on wire rack.

4. Remove side of pan; transfer cake to platter. Sprinkle with powdered sugar; serve with berries, if desired.

MAKES 10 SERVINGS

Calories: 139
Total Fat: 3 g
Saturated Fat: <1 g
Protein: 4
Carbohydrate: 25 g
Cholesterol: 42 mg
Fiber: 1 g
Sodium: 176 mg

Dietary Exchanges:
½ Fat, 1½ Starch

Carrot Cake with Cream Cheese Glaze

Reduced-fat and fat-free sour creams make a guilt-free glaze.

CAKE

- 2 cups cake flour
- 2 teaspoons ground cinnamon
- 1 teaspoon baking powder
- 1 teaspoon baking soda
- 1 teaspoon salt
- ¾ cup sugar substitute*
- ¾ cup packed brown sugar
- ¼ cup vegetable oil
- 1 cup cholesterol-free egg substitute
- ½ cup reduced-fat sour cream
- 3 cups grated carrots

GLAZE

- ½ cup (4 ounces) fat-free cream cheese, softened
- ¼ cup reduced-fat sour cream
- 1 tablespoon fat-free (skim) milk
- 1 teaspoon vanilla
- ½ cup powdered sugar

*This recipe was tested using sucralose-based sugar substitute.

1. Preheat oven to 350°F. Coat 12-cup (10-inch) bundt pan with nonstick cooking spray. Combine flour, cinnamon, baking powder, baking soda and salt in medium bowl.

2. Beat sugar substitute, brown sugar and oil in large bowl with electric mixer at medium speed. Beat in egg substitute and sour cream. Slowly add flour mixture, beating at low speed just until blended. Stir in carrots. Pour batter into prepared pan.

3. Bake about 50 minutes or until toothpick inserted near center comes out clean. Let stand 5 minutes. Invert cake onto wire rack; cool completely.

4. For glaze, whisk cream cheese, sour cream, milk and vanilla in small bowl until smooth. Whisk in powdered sugar. If glaze is too thick, add water, 1 tablespoon at a time. Spoon glaze over top and sides of cake.

MAKES 16 SERVINGS

Calories: 176, Total Fat: 5 g, Saturated Fat: 1 g, Protein: 5 g, Carbohydrate: 28 g, Cholesterol: 5 mg, Fiber: 1 g, Sodium: 357 mg

Dietary Exchanges: ½ Fat, 2 Starch

Grandma's Fig Cake

Figs are rich in fiber and make a perfect filling for a mouthwatering cake.

1 cup buttermilk

⅔ cup canola or vegetable oil

¾ cup cholesterol-free egg substitute

1 teaspoon vanilla

1½ cups sugar

2 cups flour, plus additional to sprinkle pan

1 teaspoon baking soda

1 teaspoon ground cinnamon

1 teaspoon ground allspice

½ cup toasted chopped pecans

10 dried whole figs, chopped and rehydrated*

SAUCE

½ cup buttermilk

½ teaspoon baking soda

1 cup sugar substitute**

¼ cup margarine

*To rehydrate figs, add them to 1 cup boiling water. Cover with plastic wrap and steep for 5 minutes. Drain and remove figs.

**This recipe was tested using sucralose-based sugar substitute.

1. Preheat oven to 300°F. Whisk buttermilk, oil, egg substitute and vanilla in large bowl.

2. Sift next 5 ingredients together in small bowl and add to buttermilk mixture. Mix well and add nuts and figs.

3. Pour into bundt pan liberally coated with nonstick cooking spray and sprinkled with additional flour. Bake 1 hour. Remove from oven and let stand on wire rack to cool 15 minutes. Use knife to remove and release cake from pan.

4. To make sauce, combine buttermilk, baking soda and sugar substitute in small saucepan over medium-high heat. Stir until mixture slightly thickens. Add margarine and stir until melted. Remove from heat and let cool completely. Pour over cake. Let sauce settle then cut cake into pieces.

MAKES 20 SERVINGS

Calories: 231, Total Fat: 12 g, Saturated Fat: 2 g, Protein: 3 g, Carbohydrate: 30 g, Cholesterol: 1 mg, Dietary Fiber: 1 g, Sodium: 158 mg

Dietary Exchanges: 2 Fat, 2 Starch

Index

Beef, Pork & Lamb

Chicken & Poultry

Fish & Seafood

Vegetarian

Metric Conversion Chart

VOLUME MEASUREMENTS (dry)

1/8 teaspoon = 0.5 mL
1/4 teaspoon = 1 mL
1/2 teaspoon = 2 mL
3/4 teaspoon = 4 mL
1 teaspoon = 5 mL
1 tablespoon = 15 mL
2 tablespoons = 30 mL
1/4 cup = 60 mL
1/3 cup = 75 mL
1/2 cup = 125 mL
2/3 cup = 150 mL
3/4 cup = 175 mL
1 cup = 250 mL
2 cups = 1 pint = 500 mL
3 cups = 750 mL
4 cups = 1 quart = 1 L

VOLUME MEASUREMENTS (fluid)

1 fluid ounce (2 tablespoons) = 30 mL
4 fluid ounces (1/2 cup) = 125 mL
8 fluid ounces (1 cup) = 250 mL
12 fluid ounces (1 1/2 cups) = 375 mL
16 fluid ounces (2 cups) = 500 mL

WEIGHTS (mass)

1/2 ounce = 15 g
1 ounce = 30 g
3 ounces = 90 g
4 ounces = 120 g
8 ounces = 225 g
10 ounces = 285 g
12 ounces = 360 g
16 ounces = 1 pound = 450 g

DIMENSIONS

1/16 inch = 2 mm
1/8 inch = 3 mm
1/4 inch = 6 mm
1/2 inch = 1.5 cm
3/4 inch = 2 cm
1 inch = 2.5 cm

OVEN TEMPERATURES

250°F = 120°C
275°F = 140°C
300°F = 150°C
325°F = 160°C
350°F = 180°C
375°F = 190°C
400°F = 200°C
425°F = 220°C
450°F = 230°C

BAKING PAN SIZES

Utensil	Size in Inches/Quarts	Metric Volume	Size in Centimeters
Baking or Cake Pan (square or rectangular)	8×8×2	2 L	20×20×5
	9×9×2	2.5 L	23×23×5
	12×8×2	3 L	30×20×5
	13×9×2	3.5 L	33×23×5
Loaf Pan	8×4×3	1.5 L	20×10×7
	9×5×3	2 L	23×13×7
Round Layer Cake Pan	8×1½	1.2 L	20×4
	9×1½	1.5 L	23×4
Pie Plate	8×1¼	750 mL	20×3
	9×1¼	1 L	23×3
Baking Dish or Casserole	1 quart	1 L	—
	1½ quarts	1.5 L	—
	2 quarts	2 L	—